VGM Opportunities Series

OPPORTUNITIES IN
WELDING CAREERS

Mark Rowh

Foreword by
Dr. Nelson Wall
Deputy Executive Director
American Welding Society

VGM Career Horizons
NTC/Contemporary Publishing Group

Cover Photo Credits:
Upper left courtesy of American Iron & Steel Institute; upper right courtesy of
Mountain View College; lower right courtesy of Lincoln Electric Company; lower
left courtesy of Manpower.

Library of Congress Cataloging-in-Publication Data

Rowh, Mark.
    Opportunities in welding careers / Mark Rowh ; foreword by Nelson
Wall.
       p.   cm. — (VGM opportunities series)
    Includes bibliographical references.
    ISBN 0-8442-4668-9 (alk. paper). — ISBN 0-8442-4669-7 (pbk. :
alk. paper)
    1. Welding—Vocational guidance. I. Title. II. Series.
TS227.7.R68   1997
671.5′2′023—dc20   96-9351
                                                    CIP

Published by VGM Career Horizons, a division of NTC Publishing Group
4255 West Touhy Avenue
Lincolnwood (Chicago), Illinois 60646-1975, U.S.A.
©1997 by NTC Publishing Group. All rights reserved.
No part of this book may be reproduced, stored in a retrieval
system, or transmitted in any form or by any means,
electronic, mechanical, photocopying, recording or otherwise,
without the prior permission of NTC Publishing Group.
Manufactured in the United States of America.

   8 9 VP 9 8 7 6 5 4 3 2

DEDICATION

This book is dedicated to the faculty of
Clemson University.

CONTENTS

Definitions. Development of welding. Advantages
of a welding career. Looking at a welding career in
greater detail.

Major welding processes. New types of welding.
Related technologies. The diversity of welding
processes.

Where welders work. Other work environments. Job
titles. Tools, supplies, and equipment used in welding.
A day in the life of a welder. Safety and welding.
Questions to ask yourself.

ABOUT THE AUTHOR

Mark Rowh is a widely published writer as well as an experienced educator in community college and vocational-technical education. A member of the administrative staff at New River Community College in Dublin, Virginia, he has also held administrative positions at Greenville Technical College in South Carolina and Bluefield State College and Parkersburg Community College in West Virginia.

In his educational career, Rowh has worked closely with a variety of technical programs. He holds a doctorate in vocational and technical education from Clemson University.

Rowh's articles on educational and management topics have appeared in more than fifty magazines. He previously contributed several books to the VGM Opportunities series and is the author of *Coping with Stress in College,* published by College Board Books.

ACKNOWLEDGMENTS

The author greatly appreciates the cooperation of the following in researching and writing this book:

American Welding Institute
American Welding Society
Greenville Technical College
International Association of Machinists and Aerospace Workers
New River Community College
Northeast State Technical Community College

FOREWORD

Careers in welding offer a wide variety of career opportunities, from production in leading-edge industries to pioneering research in world-class university laboratories. Yet, as we approach the year 2000, shortages of young people entering the welding industry persist at all levels. At production levels, the welding industry is getting only one replacement for every four who leave due to retirement or job change. From welding engineers to researchers seeking to unlock the secrets of the welding arc, comparable shortfalls are reported. The welding industry is full of opportunity.

The fact is that welding is involved in producing more than 50 percent of the gross national product in manufacturing. And as robots enter the industry, the influx of computers and space-age new materials is making the welding industry a most exciting and challenging environment.

New excitement also is coming into the welding industry as new welding and joining processes are developed, as the industry rapidly globalizes, and as professional development opportunities for welders are being introduced by the American Welding Society.

Upward mobility in the industry is unusually great. You can enter with a high school education and advance as you gain experience and continue your education. The industry, including the American Welding Society, is stepping up its support of education with increased scholarship and research grants.

Mobility also is abundant if you later choose to move into sales, application engineering, safety, design, or research. Experienced welders also have the option of training and testing to become certified welding inspectors.

Opportunities in welding careers are varied, affording you wide choices to build on your experience and education as you mature and your career goals change.

Nelson Wall
Deputy Executive Director
American Welding Society

INTRODUCTION

A decision regarding career choices should never be taken lightly. Such choices need to be made with as much information available to support them as possible.

Every career field has its own advantages and disadvantages, and welding is no different. The advantages can be significant, however, for persons with the right interests and aptitudes. This book describes an occupation that many men and women find both challenging and genuinely important. As with many other technical fields, the work performed by welders is key to a variety of industries and manufacturing efforts. At the same time, welders enjoy a wide range of work settings and job tasks.

For any reader interested in considering a welding career, this book is offered as an overview of the basic facts one needs to render a well-informed decision. It is hoped that the material provided here accurately conveys the details needed for a basic understanding of this fascinating career field.

CHAPTER 1

WELDING: AN OVERVIEW

Welding. It is one of the most important processes of modern civilization. The vital role of welding may not be apparent at first glance, but all around us the work of welders holds a key place in our lives.

Consider, for example, a trip to a large city. Whether you take a car or bus, the machine that transports you has been assembled at least in part by welding. Along the path of your journey, you will cross bridges constructed with the assistance of welders. Once you arrive at the city, the beautiful buildings stand as monuments to the work of welders and other craftspersons. And many of the components within the various buildings could not have been assembled without welding. From the elevators to fire escapes, welded materials abound.

No matter where you live, the work performed by welders affects hundreds of elements of your daily life. The electrical power that energizes homes, schools, and factories emanates from power plants constructed in part by welders.

Commercial airliners, tractor-trailer rigs, office buildings, guided missiles, and more owe a similar debt to the welding field. The list could go on and on, but the bottom line is that welding plays an extremely important part in many areas of life.

DEFINITIONS

What exactly is welding? There are different types of welding, but they all share a common definition: welding is the joining of two or more materials through heat, pressure, or a related process. The application of the welding process causes the materials to fuse together, in essence forming a single piece of material where two or more previously existed.

Welding may be involved in the construction of equipment, moving vehicles, buildings, or other items both large and small. Or it may consist of repairs or modifications to existing devices. In either case, the work requires special knowledge and equipment. The need for personnel who have this special knowledge means that individuals trained in welding continue to encounter a significant level of job demand. Welders not only have contributed in a major way to past developments but can be expected to continue their essential work for decades to come.

THE DEVELOPMENT OF WELDING

The first modern welding processes were invented a little over a hundred years ago. But long before that time, various techniques for working with metal had been developed. In fact, much of history has been defined by humans' capabilities for working with metal and other materials.

Early Metalworking

First there was the Stone Age, when men and women originally began to use technology. Of course this was very primitive, consisting largely of striking one rock against another in making stone scrapers, knives, and simple weapons. For hundreds of thousands of years, the use of metal was an unimagined possibility waiting to be discovered.

Then someone discovered copper, one of the softest and most easily worked metals, and figured out how to shape it into jewelry, cooking utensils, and other devices. Two other soft metals, gold and silver, were also found to be easily worked into various forms for jewelry and other items.

Although these metals were useful for some applications, they were too soft to be effective for many uses. A sword made of copper or gold, for example, would not be hard enough to stand up against weapons made of stone or other materials.

Development of Alloys

A partial answer to this dilemma was developed with the discovery of alloys. By combining two or more metals, early metal workers found that they could create a new metal with different characteristics from the original materials. The most important of these was bronze, an alloy of copper and tin. Early metal workers fashioned bronze into knives, swords, shields, eating utensils, and many other items. This metal made such a profound impact on civilization, in fact, that scholars have used the name Bronze Age to designate the period of history when its use became common.

Discovery of Iron and Steel

Even more important was the discovery of iron and, later, steel. When people first learned to smelt iron ore and obtain what was at that point the toughest metal ever known, they initiated a new era in human technology. Warriors equipped with weapons made of iron or steel found they had a tremendous advantage over opponents who were not, and empires formed and flourished thanks in great part to this new metal. Iron and steel were used not just in weapons but also in everyday items such as axes, knives, and other tools.

Over the centuries, the use of iron and steel became increasingly common. Medieval knights protected themselves in armor made of steel, and later, the Industrial Revolution saw an explosion of inventions, many of which depended on the use of iron, steel, and other metals. One of the most important was the railroad, which fostered the use of great quantities of metal in tracks as well as in trains themselves.

Early Welding

The first instances of actual welding occurred in the 1880s. Both in Europe and the United States, pioneers in the field developed and refined techniques for fusion welding and several related processes. Once the concept of welding had been proven workable, researchers and practicing welders continued developing new and innovative processes, leading eventually to the diversity of today's multifaceted welding field. Many of these developments came along during the early part of the twentieth century, as initiatives in other technologies were adapted for use in welding.

As with many other technical developments, the needs of warfare acted as a catalyst for improvement of welding technology, particularly in the areas of mass production. The demand for thousands of tanks, planes, ships, and other vehicles during World War II, for example, expanded the parameters of the welding profession. The same was true of postwar economic growth in the automobile industry, construction industry, and other areas of civilian as well as military life.

New Methods

Modern welding incorporates many of the principles developed earlier this century along with the latest in technological advancements. Since World War II, advances in welding have mirrored other developments in technology. The invention of the laser, for example, led to the creation of laser beam welding as an option to traditional welding methodology. Advances in various aspects of automated manufacturing have contributed to improvements in welding machines designed to perform assembly-line work and other increasingly automated tasks. The growing use of new kinds of plastics has precipitated the development of techniques for welding plastics. General advances in physics and electronics have contributed to varied welding applications such as electron beam welding and the use of ultrasonic welding machines.

Thanks to scores of scientific and technological breakthroughs, welding continues to be a field where new techniques add to traditional capabilities. The result is a field where existing workers do not tend to find themselves being bypassed by advancing technology. Instead, they realize enhancements in their work that make the field more diverse than ever before.

New Applications

Not only have new methods of welding emerged in recent years, but many new applications for welding have come about. America's space program, for example, depends on the work of welders in constructing rocket boosters, launch structures, and other related equipment. The creation of military and civilian aircraft has likewise become increasingly sophisticated. The construction of nuclear power plants is another area where practices perfected over the last few decades are being applied. In virtually all sectors of modern civilization, welders play some kind of role, whether that means constructing habitats for working and living or building and repairing important equipment.

Welding Techniques

Today's welders can choose from among a variety of techniques. They might utilize the relatively simple technology involved in *gas welding,* where a special torch is used to burn a gas such as acetylene, producing a flame that is hot enough to melt metal. In this process, welders usually hold the torch and complete the work by hand.

Welders also carry out *arc welding,* where instead of creating heat through combustion of gases, high temperatures are achieved through an electric arc. Here, the welder generally uses a generator to produce electric current and a welding rod or electrode to create the necessary electric arc. A number of different methods can be used to practice arc welding.

Another technique is known as *resistance welding.* Instead of an arc, electricity is controlled to create resistance as it flows between pieces of metal, fusing them together.

Still other types of welding take advantage of recent developments in other fields. Some of these modern techniques are based on such advanced technologies as lasers, electron beams, and waves of ultrasound.

More details about the major welding processes are provided in Chapter 2. The main point to remember here, though, is that welding is truly a diverse field. The act of welding might involve the manual use of a welding torch and portable gas tanks. Or it might mean the operation of a complicated automated welding machine. Being employed as a welder can mean working for an automobile factory, the government, a large construction company, or a small welding shop. The person who becomes a welder might take a job in his or her home town or might end up helping construct an electric plant in Africa or an oil rig in the Gulf of Mexico. With so many options, a career in welding can certainly provide a wide range of possibilities.

ADVANTAGES OF A WELDING CAREER

Those who pursue a career in welding choose this field for a variety of reasons. Among them are the following advantages.

The Satisfaction of Performing Skilled Work

If you have ever held a part-time job or other employment, you know that working has its good and bad points.

Every job features both ups and downs, but not every kind of work provides satisfaction in accomplishing the tasks at hand. This is especially true for many jobs that require no special skills or training. For instance, some workers find it hard to derive satisfaction from such jobs as collecting garbage, standing and holding signs for a highway construction crew, or cleaning motel rooms. This is not to say that there is anything wrong with such positions or the people who hold them, but it is not unusual to find that those working in such jobs obtain little pleasure from performing them.

A job such as welding, on the other hand, often provides a more satisfying work experience. After all, welders perform detailed work that a person who has not had the right training simply cannot do. The fact that special skills are needed helps boost a sense of accomplishment in work that requires skill, patience, and diligence.

Moreover, there is something inherently satisfying in the building process itself. Working in cooperation with other craftspersons, welders help construct some of the largest and most advanced structures known to the world. Can you imagine watching the christening of a huge aircraft carrier or merchant ship and knowing that you helped construct it? Or on a less grandiose scale, how do you think it would feel to do a good job of building or repairing a small appliance? In either case, the act of constructing something useful or making a key repair to an item of value can provide a genuine measure of satisfaction.

The Right Type of Work Setting

A popular rock song from the 1970s touts the philosophy of "different strokes for different folks," referring to the old truism that people have different likes and dislikes. This is as true in the area of careers as in anything else. Some people love to sit at a desk and manipulate words or figures all day; for others, such a job would be tremendously boring. Some people prefer to work indoors, while others enjoy putting in their hours outside whenever possible. Still others like to supervise people more than any other function.

Depending on your own preferences, a career in welding may provide just the right environment. If working in an office does not sound appealing, the basic hands-on approach involved in welding might be more suitable. Of course, job environments vary according to the type of welding being performed, but the range of possibilities can include working outdoors, on the floor of a factory, or in a small shop setting. In fact, some welders (such as those in building construction) move frequently from one job site to the next, encountering many different job environments.

If your idea of the right job involves wearing a three-piece suit or fancy dress to work every day and making your living from behind a desk, then a welding career probably does not represent a smart choice. If, on the other hand, you enjoy working with equipment and have a flair for building things, this field may be ideal for you. A welding career can allow you the chance to work in a setting where you feel unfettered by office politics, the need to maintain an expensive wardrobe, or other restrictions found in many careers.

Good Pay and Benefits

Welders earn good pay, and that is a major point of attraction for many workers. As discussed more fully in later chapters, welders earn higher-than-average wages around the country. Persons willing to invest a modest amount of time in a welding training program almost always find that their efforts pay off many times over.

Most welding jobs also include a variety of fringe benefits, such as medical insurance, retirement plans, and other important support. In many instances, these benefits are provided through a union contract, where a labor union has worked intensively to gain the best possible package of wages and benefits for its members. Even in nonunion environments, however, welders usually earn good benefits as well as attractive wages.

A Field That Should Not Become Outdated

With the rapid changes in contemporary life, a major consideration in any career decision must be its potential for the future. Too often, careers that sound promising today become obsolete when some new technology explodes on the scene.

Of course no guarantees can be issued for any field, but experts in welding feel a need for this process will continue on a long-term basis. According to the American Welding Society, there are currently over 420,000 welders employed in the United States alone, along with about 60,000 welding supervisors. And job openings are expected to expand through 2005.

Technological advancements may change the way in which many welding processes are conducted, but welding itself will continue to be important. Tomorrow's welders may be constructing components for a space station or a new type of ocean-going vehicle, among other things, but they will still be welding a variety of metals and other materials. For many years to come, men and women skilled in applying welding techniques are projected to be needed in a variety of manufacturing fields and other areas.

The American Welding Society has noted these advantages of a welding career:

- Job opportunities immediately after high school (with vocational-technical studies)
- Opportunities for growth through new and emerging technologies
- A variety of jobs and duties
- Job security based on a skill needed for national production
- Competitive wages
- Opportunities for jobs in a variety of locations

LOOKING AT A WELDING CAREER
IN GREATER DETAIL

The remainder of this book provides an overview of various factors involved in a career in welding. Chapter 2 looks at the major welding processes. Chapter 3 covers typical jobs performed by welders and the variety in working environments. In Chapter 4, you will find an overview of the educational process needed to prepare for a welding career, along with tips for negotiating the educational process. Chapter 5 discusses special programs where training can be obtained, while Chapter 6 covers organizations and certifications. Earnings and benefits are covered in Chapter 7. The range of opportunities in the field is noted in Chapter 8, and tips on getting started in welding are covered in Chapter 9.

In addition, three helpful appendices are included to provide you with additional information for possible use in considering or planning for a welding career. All told, the book provides a detailed look at welding careers and how you might fit in. Read on, and you may find that a welding career offers something for you.

CHAPTER 2

CONTEMPORARY WELDING

Although welding has been a key process for decades, it is by no means a technology of the past. Welding continues to play an important part in contemporary manufacturing efforts. As times have changed, so have the methods used in the practice of welding.

MAJOR WELDING PROCESSES

Welding offers a great deal of diversity. In fact, there are more than 80 different types of welding and allied processes, according to the American Welding Society. Some welders will use only one of these techniques while others will master many. The type of welding used depends on the equipment available, the job being performed, and the training of the individual welder.

If you become a welder, you will learn in depth the characteristics of one or more of these processes. What follows is a brief description of the major welding techniques, which can be divided into several basic categories: arc welding, gas welding, resistance welding, soldering, brazing, solid-state welding, and other processes.

The most common welding processes, including arc and gas methods, fall within the umbrella of *fusion welding*. Here, heat is used to melt metals or other materials. The heat may be generated in any one of several ways. Once molten, the materials mix together and then become fused as they cool. Thus, two steel rods or beams, for example, can become essentially one piece of metal. In many cases, a filler material is also used in the process. This filler is heated, and as it becomes molten, it fills the joint between the original materials (called base metals or base materials).

Welding techniques vary in a number of ways. The most important differences include the way in which heat is produced, the type of fillers used (if any), the type of gas used for creating heat or providing shielding from contamination (if any), and the degree of automation.

Oxyfuel Gas Welding

If you had never tried welding but were asked to describe it, this is probably the methodology you would envision. In this type of welding, heat is produced by burning two gases: oxygen and another gas such as acetylene. The two gases are stored in heavy metal cylinders, which are connected to a welding torch by flexible hoses. The welder releases a stream of gas from each cylinder through a controlling device known as a regulator, and the two streams flow together inside the welding torch. As the gases begin to flow, the welder makes a spark or otherwise ignites the mixture, directs the flame to the area to be welded, and begins the welding process. This consists of using the flame to melt the base materials and then adding filler material as needed. All this is normally done by hand rather than through any kind of automated equipment.

The most common process of this type is *oxyacetylene welding*. This is often the preferred method of gas welding because burning acetylene produces a higher temperature than other gases used in welding. When burned after mixing with oxygen (which makes the gas burn more rapidly and at a higher temperature), acetylene can produce temperatures exceeding 5000 degrees Fahrenheit or 3000 degrees Celsius.

This type of welding can also be performed with other gases. Hydrogen, for example, can be mixed with oxygen in the same manner. Other gases such as methane, propane, and several others, which produce lower temperatures, are used for work related to welding such as metal cutting.

An advantage of oxyfuel welding is that it is a fairly simple process. Only a minimum of equipment is needed, and it can be moved about easily by a single welder. Thus, the process can be provided almost anywhere and is less expensive than more elaborate methods.

A disadvantage of oxyfuel welding is that it can be used for only certain types of jobs. Since the heat produced by burning gases is not as great as with some other methods, applications are limited to materials with relatively low melting points. In addition, the work proceeds more slowly than with many other methods. In general, it is not effective for large-scale jobs or those requiring speed or high volume.

Arc Welding

SMAW

One of the most common types of welding is *shielded metal arc welding* (often designated as SMAW). This is usually a manual process where the welder grasps a holder that contains a covered electrode used to create an electric arc. The welder turns on a welding machine, which then causes electric current to flow to the electrode. As the electricity jumps across the gap between the tip of the electrode and the base material, it forms an arc that is hot enough to melt the electrode tip and the base material and form a weld.

The term *shielded* refers to a layer of gas that is released by the electrode covering when it becomes hot. This gas protects the weld from being contaminated by the various elements of the atmosphere.

As the welder manipulates the electrode, it gradually melts away and provides filler material. Thus, electrodes must be continually replaced as a routine part of SMAW. Many different types of electrodes are available, varying in size, type of coating, usefulness in welding specific kinds of metals, and other characteristics. A major part of the experienced welder's job can be choosing the right electrode for the situation at hand.

GTAW

Another arc welding method is *gas tungsten arc welding* (GTAW). Here, a gas shield is provided not by a covered electrode as in SMAW, but instead by a cylinder of gas. The gas is not burned in this case. It is an inert gas used to surround the area being welded and keep it from being contaminated by the different gases that make up the atmosphere. Inert gases (such as argon and helium) provide an effective shield because they do not normally react chemically with other elements.

In the GTAW process, a welding machine produces heat by creating an electric arc between an electrode made of tungsten and the area being welded. Tungsten has a high melting point; it does not become molten during GTAW welding. If filler material is needed to form the weld, it is periodically inserted into the arc by a two-hand technique.

This type of welding is also called TIG welding (for tungsten inert gas). It is often used for welding aluminum and stainless steel, among other metals.

GMAW

In *gas metal arc welding* (GMAW), the electrode, instead of being made of tungsten, is a continuous length of wire with a relatively low melting point, matching the properties of the metal to be welded. Generally, this wire is fed automatically by a welding machine, passing through a welding gun and serving as filler material at the point where the weld occurs.

In some cases, this process is completely automated, with the positioning of the welding gun also controlled by machine rather than by hand. In manual welding, the process of feeding wire is controlled by machine, but a welder manipulates the welding gun itself and directs the application of wire.

GMAW processes are also referred to as MIG welding (for metal inert gas). This type of welding is effective with a wide variety of materials.

Other types of arc welding include the following:

- Plasma Arc Welding (PAW). Here, an electric arc creates "plasma" by heating any one of several gases to an extremely high temperature. The heated gas is then directed to a tightly controlled area where it melts the base metal to be welded.
- Flux Cored Arc Welding (FCAW). This process is similar to gas metal arc welding, with the difference that the electrode consists of hollow wire that is filled with a flexing material to provide shielding of the molten electrode and base metal during welding.
- Carbon Arc Welding (CAW). This welding technique uses electrodes made of carbon. In some cases, the arc is created between a carbon electrode and the base material, while in others the arc bridges two carbon electrodes.

- Submerged Arc Welding (SAW). As the name implies, submerged arc welding involves covering the arc during the welding process. This is accomplished by submerging the weld area under a granular flux. The welder does not actually see the area being welded, but instead controls it by machine through an automatic or semiautomatic process.

Resistance Welding

Resistance welding (RW) is an electric welding process, whereby an electric current forced to pass through a poor conductor is converted to heat by the resistance of the medium. In resistance welding, electricity is passed through two pieces of metal in contact to heat the metal at the interface, and the two pieces are pressed together after they have fused. Once cooled, the parts have become welded together.

Employers who use the resistance method may assign welders to several different types of resistance welding equipment. These include:

- Flash welding (FW), where parts being welded are brought into contact and briefly separated to create an electric arc, and then quickly pressed together, causing sparks, or "flashes," for which the process is named.
- Percussion welding (PEW), where parts are percussively forced together during or immediately following an electrical discharge.

- Resistance spot welding (RSW), in which opposing electrodes heat one spot at the facing surfaces between metal sheets to be joined, with heat supplied by electric current.
- Resistance seam welding (RSW), a process using a series of overlapping spot welds to produce a watertight or airtight seam.
- Resistance projection welding (RPW), where projections, embossments, or intersections are raised on the work parts to localize predetermined weld points.
- Upset welding (UW), in which pieces of metal are clamped together and joined through the resistance to electric current.

Brazing

Brazing is similar to welding, but it differs from most welding processes in that the objects or materials being joined are not melted. Instead, a different substance with a lower melting point from the materials to be joined is melted and used to join them together. The basic concept of brazing might be compared to using glue to join together two objects.

For example, brazing can be used to join together copper tubes or pipes. A filler metal with a relatively low melting point, such as brass (an alloy of zinc and copper), is heated with a torch and applied to the copper pieces, joining them together as the alloy melts and then solidifies.

Although heat is used, only the filler material becomes molten. As a result, brazing can be used to join materials that must be treated delicately (such as gems or jewelry) as well as copper pipes, aluminum, and many other materials.

Soldering

Soldering is somewhat similar to brazing. A major difference is that a still lower temperature is used in the process, meaning that quite different filler materials are applied. In many cases, the filler is an alloy of tin and lead. Such an alloy melts easily and requires only a simple device known as a soldering iron for application. Many people learn soldering as their first exposure to any welding-related process, often in connection with work in electronics. In industrial applications, soldering is used for jobs ranging from joining tubes inside an air conditioner to attaching parts of sophisticated electronic devices.

Although soldering is readily done by hand, many industrial soldering jobs are handled automatically with several types of soldering machines.

Solid-State Welding

Until just a few generations ago, one of the most important persons in any community was the blacksmith. Blacksmiths were among the precursors of today's welders, for as a part of their jobs, they were able to join pieces of metal together. Blacksmiths learned to heat metal until it became more malleable (even though it did not melt) and then hammered the pieces together. This form of forge welding is still practiced by blacksmiths today, although the craft may soon become a largely forgotten skill. The same approach is also used in more modern manufacturing processes, where special furnaces heat metal devices that are then fused together.

Even when metals are not heated, some can be joined together through a process known as cold welding. Softer metals such as aluminum, lead, silver, and gold can be fused together by applying sufficient pressure.

Several other types of solid-state welding are also used in a variety of applications, including diffusion welding, friction welding, and a number of variations.

NEW TYPES OF WELDING

In any area of technology advancements inevitably occur, and welding is no different. During recent years, several new welding processes have been introduced, and more can be expected in the future.

Lasers

One of the most interesting of the newer processes is *laser beam welding* (LBW). As the name indicates, this type of welding depends on the highly amplified beams of light (lasers) that are now used commonly in a number of applications. Although many laser applications depend on the beams passing through or bouncing harmlessly off material (as with the scanning devices used at checkout counters in grocery stores), for use in welding, laser beams are quite intensive and capable of producing great heat. With a laser welding machine (a complex and expensive piece of equipment), a tightly controlled beam of light is produced that can melt many metals quickly.

A plus for LBW is that it can be very precise. The area heated is tiny, resulting in the potential for extremely accurate work. This can be important in scientific and highly technical applications.

Electron Beams

Another innovative process is *electron beam welding* (EBW). In this process, a stream of electrons (charged particles that are one of the basic parts of atoms) is produced by heating a filament. The high-velocity electrons are focused near the point to be welded, which is usually placed inside a chamber where all the air has been removed to create a vacuum. This produces heat that is so intense portions of the metal are vaporized and condense on the opposite wall of the "vapor hole." The beam pierces through the metal as it progresses along the weld joint.

Ultrasonics

Unlike most welding techniques, ultrasonic welding does not use or produce heat. Instead, the welder operates a machine that produces intense sound vibrations. These high-frequency sound waves break up the surface of the materials being joined together and then cause them to fuse.

Ultrasonic welding is particularly useful in producing electronic devices and components. It is also used extensively in packaging food and beverages.

Other Advancements

Other welding processes offer their own unique features. Some differ substantially from traditional welding methods, while others combine features of two or more processes. Such processes as electrogas welding, electroslag welding, friction welding, and diffusion welding also provide alternative approaches for accomplishing various welding tasks. A complete listing of the major welding processes is provided later in this chapter.

RELATED TECHNOLOGIES

The aim of welders is to join materials together for the purposes of construction or repair. The basic skills and aptitudes required in welding, however, can also be applied to the cutting of metal and other metalworking functions.

A variety of welding methods may be employed by welders or by persons who specialize in cutting as opposed to welding (with the difference being that welding generally entails joining materials together while cutting involves just the opposite). Of course, these functions can be closely related, as when workers must cut off a section of metal from a larger piece and then weld it to another. On the other hand, and depending on the job, cutting may consist entirely of taking apart materials or structures.

At any rate, a variety of techniques may be used in cutting. Thermal cutting techniques depend on using oxygen or electric arc processes, while other methods include laser beam cutting and electron beam cutting.

Still other processes related to welding include thermal spraying (a method of metal resurfacing) and an alternative method of joining materials known as adhesive bonding.

THE DIVERSITY OF WELDING PROCESSES

The previous pages have provided a brief overview of some of the most important welding processes and those that are used most commonly today. Many other related processes, however, also have their own individual applications.

Below is a list of welding and related processes as reported by the American Welding Society (AWS). This information is adapted with permission from the AWS publication *Standard Welding Terms and Definitions.*

ARC WELDING

atomic hydrogen welding	AHW
bare metal arc welding	BMAW
carbon arc welding	CAW
gas	CAW-G
shielded	CAW-S
twin	CAW-T
electrogas welding	EGW
flux cored arc welding	FCAW
gas metal arc welding	GMAW
pulsed arc	GMAW-P
short circuiting arc	GMAW-S
gas tungsten arc welding	GTAW
pulsed arc	GTAW-P
plasma arc welding	PAW
shielded metal arc welding	SMAW
stud arc welding	SW
submerged arc welding	SAW
series	SAW-S

OXYFUEL GAS WELDING (OFW)

air acetylene welding	AAW
oxyacetylene welding	OAW
oxyhydrogen welding	OHW
pressure gas welding	PGW

RESISTANCE WELDING (RW)

flash welding	FW
high frequency resistance welding	HFRW

percussion welding	PEW
projection welding	RPW
resistance seam welding	RSEW
resistance spot welding	RSW
upset welding	UW

SOLID-STATE WELDING (SSW)

coextrusion welding	CEW
cold welding	CW
diffusion welding	DFW
explosion welding	EXW
forge welding	FOW
friction welding	FRW
hot pressure welding	HPW
roll welding	ROW
ultrasonic welding	USW

BRAZING (B)

arc brazing	AB
block brazing	BB
diffusion brazing	DFB
dip brazing	DB
flow brazing	FLB
furnace brazing	FB
induction brazing	IB
infrared brazing	IRB
resistance brazing	RB
torch brazing	TB
twin carbon arc blazing	TCAB

SOLDERING (S)

dip soldering	DS
furnace soldering	FS
induction soldering	IS
infrared soldering	IRS
iron soldering	INS
resistance soldering	RS
torch soldering	TS
wave soldering	WS

OTHER WELDING

electron beam welding	EBW
high vacuum	EBW-HV
medium vacuum	EBW-MV
nonvacuum	EBW-NV
electroslag welding	ESW
flow welding	FLOW
induction welding	IW
laser beam welding	LBW
thermit welding	TW

PROCESSES ALLIED TO WELDING

THERMAL SPRAYING (THSP)

electric arc spraying	EASP
flame spraying	FLSP
plasma spraying	PSP

ADHESIVE BONDING (ABD)

OXYGEN CUTTING (OC)

chemical flux cutting	FOC
metal powder cutting	POC

oxyfuel gas cutting	OFC
oxyacatylene cutting	OFC-A
oxyhydrogen cutting	OFC-H
oxynatural gas cutting	OFC-N
oxypropane cutting	OFC-P
oxygen cutting	AOC
oxygen lance cutting	LOC

ARC CUTTING (AC)

air carbon arc cutting	AAC
carbon arc cutting	CAC
gas metal arc cutting	GMAC
gas tungsten arc cutting	GTAC
metal arc cutting	MAC
plasma arc cutting	PAC
shielded metal arc cutting	SMAC

OTHER CUTTING

electron beam cutting	EBC
laser beam cutting	LBC

At first glance, such a long list of welding processes may be a little intimidating. But when you consider the following points, the depth and breadth of the welding field can seem substantially less overpowering.

You will need to learn only a few of these processes, or perhaps just one. Many welding jobs focus on just one type of welding work. Unless you change jobs frequently or simply want to learn all kinds of processes, you probably will not be required to master a wide range of techniques.

There is always more to learn. Because the field is so diverse, the opportunity to learn more always exists. This can provide a great way to avoid boredom on the job, as well as open up areas for you to advance yourself professionally.

Welding always offers room for new technologies and new materials. Because welding grows and changes along with other technologies, it does not become easily outdated. This is an extremely important point for those concerned about job security in future years. By changing and growing, the welding field remains a strong, viable area of employment.

CHAPTER 3

THE WORK OF WELDERS

As the previous chapter illustrates, the work performed by welders can vary widely. Welders construct all kinds of items. They may use a simple welding torch or a complex machine costing over a million dollars. They may work on their own or in teams, entirely by hand or only with automated equipment. One welder may do the same kind of work day in and day out, while another may switch frequently from one job assignment to another.

Although persons employed in welding may work in diverse environments, they share a number of common factors. All welders use their particular skills to construct or repair buildings, equipment, or other man-made structures. In most cases, this involves working with metal, although in recent years welding has also expanded into plastics and other materials. In any case, most welders approach their jobs in similar ways, and they work within a few basic areas. While one welder may specialize in using equipment that is unfamiliar to another, the basic kind of work done is quite similar from one industry to another, from East Coast to

West Coast, whether in urban or rural areas. Even in other countries, the tasks performed by welders tend to be somewhat similar, especially when grouped within basic areas of welding technology as described in the previous chapter.

WHERE WELDERS WORK

Building Construction

If you see a new house being constructed in your neighborhood, the workers probably will not include welders. Although some of the basic components may have involved welding (for example, the construction of furnaces or certain kinds of plumbing fixtures), other work is performed by different craftspersons.

For other types of buildings, however, welders may play an important role in the construction process. For example, a highrise office building will not be made of wood and brick. Instead it is more likely to be constructed largely of steel and reinforced concrete. Much of the steel superstructure of the building will be assembled by welders. Before any concrete can be poured, welders or other metalworkers must connect beams and weld together the steel reinforcing rods.

The same is true in the construction of other large buildings. A gymnasium might be built of any number of materials, but a basic part of its construction will be metal beams and various elements of the basic support structure. A single-level manufacturing building might be constructed of corrugated metal designed for fast construction and a "no-frills" work environment—with welders performing much of the basic assembly. Or a car dealership might be expanding into a new series of buildings including a new showroom, repair shop, and office facilities—all containing substantial quantities of metal components that must be assembled by welders.

The fact that welding is an important facet of the construction industry means that opportunities for welders abound in all kinds of settings. In virtually every city in America, a quick trip across town will reveal a number of buildings under construction. The same is true in suburban areas and even many rural communities, especially where industrial parks are located. And the majority of these construction jobs call for the work of welders.

An interesting aspect of building construction is that many structures are partially or entirely prefabricated. In these cases, welders and other workers may turn out a variety of building components (or even entire structures such as storage buildings) without ever leaving their shop environment.

On the other hand, working on the site of a new building can provide an interesting challenge for the welder. Persons employed in such positions often cite the change in routine from one building project to the next as a major asset of their jobs.

Bridge/Highway Construction

The next time you take a drive in a car or truck, pay special attention to the presence of metal within the highway systems you are travelling on. While at first glance it appears that highways are made entirely of concrete or asphalt, almost every road construction project also involves the placement of metal in a variety of locations—from guard rails to huge bridges spanning rivers or valleys. In addition, many smaller bridges are built into roads that are not particularly obvious to the traveler.

The construction of bridges represents one of the most intensive and important applications of modern welding processes. Welders help construct long bridges for interstate highways and state roads, small bridges crossing country streams, and everything in between. With the growth in population and the building of new highways, bridge construction continues to be a major area in which welders work. In addition, bridges are not permanent—even though they may last for decades—and the repair and replacement of worn-out bridges calls for the help of welders.

Automotive Industry

The automobile industry is one of the largest business endeavors in North America. Every year, according to the *World Almanac and Book of Facts,* more than 9 million cars and trucks are manufactured in the United States, and nearly

2 million in Canada. In the manufacturing of all these automobiles, welders play an important part. Since most cars are largely made of metal, welding is an essential step in making most auto components.

Frequently, the welding process in car and truck construction is an automated one. Many workers in large auto plants become operators of welding machines. Although this work is important and yields good wages and benefits, it may not require in-depth knowledge of a variety of welding techniques. This may be seen as an advantage for those who enjoy mastering a single job and then sticking to it. On the other hand, it could be perceived as a disadvantage to those who prefer a great deal of variety in the workplace.

As technology continues to advance, more steps in the construction of automobiles are being carried out by robots and other devices. Nevertheless, a welding robot needs to be supervised by a knowledgeable welder. In addition, a greater reliance on plastics and composite materials will reduce the need for welding in basic car construction.

The auto repair industry represents another area where welding is important. While this is largely the province of auto mechanics, mechanics welcome the speed and simplicity of welding. For example, a broken radiator or exhaust pipe may need to be repaired, with welding being the most practical method. Or say that an individual wants to add a hitch to his or her car for towing a camper, boat, or trailer. A hitch for this purpose may be constructed or adapted by a worker who specializes in welding such parts.

Work in auto repairing is where some people first learn welding. Auto repair can also be the starting point for a career in other types of welding applications.

Shipbuilding

Although there are not nearly as many ships produced annually as cars or airplanes, the huge amount of work involved in constructing a ship still creates an enormous demand for the skills of welders. In fact, shipbuilding is one of the major areas of employment for welders.

Compared with the manufacture of planes or autos, the scope and scale of shipbuilding are vastly larger. Welders may be involved for months or years in the construction of a single ship. Instead of the finished product being an automobile that weighs less than two tons, the end result may be a merchant vessel or naval ship that spans the length of a football field and weighs thousands of tons. Building a supertanker or aircraft carrier, for example, may be more akin to constructing a small city than simply assembling a means of transportation.

At any rate, the large amounts of metal used in building ships means that the work of welders is required in a major way. Many welders spend all of their time solely in this industry.

Naturally, most welding jobs related to shipbuilding are found in coastal areas such as the Norfolk-Hampton Roads area in Virginia. Persons interested in working as welders in this industry should either live within commuting distance of major ship construction facilities or be willing to relocate to such an area on a temporary or permanent basis.

This applies to the actual assembly of ships, but not necessarily to all their components. As with many other industries, companies that build ships rely on other firms for many elements of the finished product. In many cases, welding jobs at inland locations are also involved in shipbuilding. For instance, key ship parts may be built at a factory far from the ocean and then transported to the ship construction site. So, at least indirectly, welding jobs based on ship construction may be obtained at various locations around the country.

Furthermore, some vessels are not designed to travel at sea but rather on inland waterways. Large barges that carry coal and other items on waterways such as the Ohio River and Mississippi River may be constructed far from any ocean, but involve many of the same kinds of welding work as in ocean-going ship construction.

Aircraft Construction

As with cars and ships, airplanes are constructed largely of metal parts, and the aerospace industry relies heavily on the work of welders and other metal workers. Welders help construct jumbo jets and other commercial airliners, midsized planes for commercial and private use, and many small airplanes and helicopters. In addition, they help meet the needs of the armed forces by building military aircraft, often under the employment of a private corporation that has been awarded a defense contract.

Because of the stringent safety measures observed in the aircraft industry, the work performed by welders in this area provides special challenges. Welders employed in this capacity must provide consistently good work that meets corporate and federal safety and performance standards.

The sheer beauty and excitement many people feel when working with modern flying machines can also be enjoyed by those who build them. It is difficult not to feel a sense of accomplishment in helping construct craft that can fly faster than sound, hover virtually motionless just off the ground, or perform any of the other functions possible with various types of airplanes and helicopters. As a result, working in the aircraft industry can be one of the more glamorous welding careers.

OTHER WORK ENVIRONMENTS

In many cases, individuals who have been trained as welders can also find employment in related areas. This might involve working for a period of years as a welder and then changing to a related area. Or it might mean studying welding to learn basic concepts and then following a career in one of the following areas.

Welding Sales

A career closely related to welding is the sale of welding products. While a salesperson need not necessarily be a trained welder, men and women with some experience in welding can be expected to have an edge in understanding the products they sell and the particular needs of customers. Thus, a career track that a welder might follow is branching off into the sale of equipment and supplies for the welding industry.

Pick up any telephone directory and look in the yellow pages under "welding equipment and supplies," and you will see a number of companies. The Norfolk-Portsmouth area in Virginia, for example, shows 14 different welding supply/equipment firms in the yellow pages alone, not counting those who choose to pass up this form of advertising. In this or any other city, the range of sales positions varies from clerks working in a branch of a large company to persons running their own small businesses.

A career in sales is certainly not for everyone, but it might be a possibility for you, especially if you can exhibit (or develop) most of the following characteristics:

- A basic understanding of welding concepts and practices
- Good oral communication skills
- A genuine liking for working with people
- A high degree of self-motivation and the ability to work independently without a great deal of supervision

- Good organizational and record-keeping abilities
- Honesty
- A willingness to travel frequently (if required, as some —but not all—sales jobs require travel)

Of course, different people handle sales positions in different ways, and there is no single formula for success. But if you can demonstrate these kinds of qualities, welding-related sales work may represent a challenging career alternative.

Teaching

If you become a skilled welder, one option worth exploring is teaching. Teaching is certainly not for everyone, but it can provide a rewarding career for some men and women who have mastered welding techniques to the degree where they would be in a realistic position to teach such skills to others.

A quick look at Appendix B will show you that hundreds of community and technical colleges offer programs in welding. In addition, many trade schools and vocational high schools offer similar programs. In each case, welding instructors are needed to teach the various courses offered.

The requirements for obtaining welding teaching positions vary depending on the type of school, local standards, rules established by accrediting agencies, and other factors. In some cases, a college degree is required; in others, experience and technical knowledge can be substituted for some educational credentials. If you are interested in teaching, check with the welding department, personnel office, or other appropriate official at any school that offers welding and ask what is expected of persons desiring to teach. You can then keep these requirements in mind as you acquire welding skills and other background.

One of the nice features of teaching is that it is not necessarily an "either-or" proposition. In other words, becoming a teacher does not mean you must give up welding work in other settings. Many welding teachers serve as instructors on a part-time basis only, teaching evening or other classes to expand their horizons and earn some extra income. Similarly, full-time welding instructors may perform direct welding work on a part-time or summer basis when it does not conflict with their educational duties.

Business Owner

Some welders choose to start their own businesses rather than work for other employers. This may mean operating what is sometimes called a "job shop," where welders perform various welding jobs for individuals, small businesses, or even large companies that contract out such work instead of hiring their own staff of welders.

Another option is to own or manage a business that specializes in welding equipment or supplies. Every company or individual conducting welding work must obtain the necessary equipment and supplies, ranging from complex welding machines to consumable supplies, such as the various gases used in oxyfuel and other welding processes. The resultant demand means that a continuing market exists for firms specializing in such products.

A degree or diploma in welding is not necessary to manage a business of this type, but basic knowledge of welding practices is essential. In addition, an understanding of the elements of business management is vital.

The Military

While most welding jobs are found with civilian companies, the skills of welders are also in significant demand within the armed services. An advantage of joining the armed services is that the military will provide the needed training at no cost to you. Such training can be applied not only during time spent in the armed services but also in civilian life following military service. Not only is the training itself free, but you earn normal military pay while being trained. Such a combination can be hard to beat.

Naturally, all of this depends on your ability to fit into military life and adapt to its particular requirements. Some people thrive in the military, while others hate it. The situation all depends on your own goals, career preferences, and basic personality. To find out more about the options provided by military service, contact a recruiter for any one of the armed forces. Then take some time to weigh things carefully before making any kind of commitment.

JOB TITLES

The U.S. Department of Labor lists scores of job titles related to welding. Among them are the following:

Arc Cutter
Gas-Tungsten Arc Cutter
Plasma Arc Cutter
Brazer
Assembler Brazer
Controlled Atmospheric Furnace Brazer
Crawler Torch Blazer
Electronic Brazer
Furnace Brazer
Furnace Brazer Helper
Induction Brazer Helper
Induction Brazer
Production Line Brazer
Repair and Salvage Brazer
Resistance Brazer
Brazing-Furnace Feeder
Brazing-Machine Feeder
Brazing-Machine Operator
Brazing-Machine Operator Helper
Brazing-Machine Setter
Hand Burner
Burning-Machine Operator
Certified Welder
Gas Cutter

Electronic-Eye-Thermal-Cutting-Machine Operator
Flame-Brazing-Machine Operator
Flame-Cutting-Machine Operator
Flame-Cutting-Machine-Operator Helper
Flame Gouger
Flame Planer
Flame Scarfer
Flash-Welding-Machine Operator
Flash Brusher
Gas-Cutting-Machine Operator
Hydrogen Brazing-Furnace Operator
Laser-Beam Cutter
Laser-Beam-Machine Operator
Lead Burner
Lead-Burner Apprentice
Lead-Burner Supervisor
Machine Feeder
Machine Helper
Magnetic-Thermal-Cutting-Machine Operator
Percussion-Welding-Machine Operator
Performance-Test Inspector
Plasma-Cutting-Machine Operator
Production-Welding-Machine Operator
Cylinder Heads Repairer
Welding Equipment Repairer
Induction-Heating-Equipment Setter
Side-Seam Tender
Slag Scraper

Solderer-Assembler
Solderer-Dipper
Electronic Solderer
Furnace Solderer
Induction Solderer
Production Line Solderer
Silver Solderer
Torch Solderer
Soldering-Machine Feeder
Soldering-Machine Operator
Soldering-Machine Operator Helper
Hand Thermal Cutter
Thermal-Cutter Helper
Thermal-Cutting-Tracer-Machine Operator
Torch Brazer
Torch Cutter
Upset-Welding-Machine Operator
Acetylene Welder
Arc Welder Apprentice
Arc Welder
Gas Welder
Gas Welder Apprentice
Combination Welder
Combination Welder Apprentice
Experimental Welder
Explosion Welder
Welder-Fitter
Welder-Fitter Apprentice

Arc Welder-Fitter
Gas Welder-Fitter
Flux-Cored Arc Welder
Gas-Metal Arc Welder
Gas-Tungsten Arc Welder
Gun Welder
Submerged Arc Hand Welder
Welder Helper
Oxyacetylene Welder
Oxyhydrogen Welder
Plasma Arc Welder
Production Line Welder
Production Line Arc Welder
Repair Welder
Electron-Beam Machine Welder Setter
Resistance Machine Welder Setter
Shielded-Metal Arc Welder
Structural Repair Welder
Tack Welder
Tool and Die Welder
Welding-Machine Feeder
Arc Welding-Machine Operator
Electro-Gas Welding-Machine Operator
Electron Beam Welding-Machine Operator
Electroslag Welding-Machine Operator
Friction Welding-Machine Operator
Gas Welding-Machine Operator

Gas-Metal Arc Welding-Machine Operator
Gas-Tungsten Arc Welding Machine Operator
Welding-Machine-Operator Helper
Submerged Arc Welding-Machine Operator
Thermit Welding-Machine Operator
Ultrasonic Welding-Machine Operator
Welding-Machine Tender
Welding Tester
Weld Inspector
Welding Supervisor

TOOLS, SUPPLIES, AND EQUIPMENT
USED IN WELDING

A requirement in any welding job is the ability to use basic equipment necessary to carry out various welding tasks. While every person employed in welding will not necessarily need to know how to use each and every type of equipment available, most welders work routinely with a wide range of tools, supplies, and welding equipment. Some of the most frequently used items include:

- Goggles—used for basic eye protection
- Protective gloves—used to protect hands and wrists
- Safety shoes—shoes containing steel toes or other safety features
- Igniter—used to create sparks to ignite flammable gases

- Gas cylinders—metal containers, usually made of steel, that contain compressed gases such as oxygen or acetylene
- Cylinder valves—devices used to release or restrict the flow of gas from a cylinder
- Welding booth—a confined area for use in welding; walls keep sparks and metal spattering from surrounding area
- Welding torch—a basic device, often hand held, from which heat is applied directly to the area being welded
- Welding positioner—a device used to position and hold materials while welding takes place
- Various types of welding machines

A DAY IN THE LIFE OF A WELDER

Perhaps there is no such thing as a typical day in the life of a welder. But to give you a more complete picture of what a career in welding might be like, here is an overview of one day's routine as followed by two persons employed as welders.

Mining Equipment Welder

Maria works for a company that makes mining equipment. She was very nervous during her first day on the job eight months ago, fearing not only that she might make some critical mistake but that she might not be accepted by the four other welders working for the same company, all of whom were male. But her co-workers were helpful and cooperative, especially when she demonstrated that she could handle the job readily.

Most of Maria's time is taken up in helping construct various kinds of mining equipment, including huge automatic mining machines known as continuous miners. Her daily work routine begins at 8:00 A.M., when she clocks in and picks up where she finished working the previous day. Unlike many employees in other manufacturing firms who work rotating shifts, Maria and the co-workers in her unit work eight-hour, daytime assignments most of the year. Occasionally, as when the company has received a high volume of business and production levels must be increased, Maria and other employees are asked to work overtime, which may consist of evening work or a Saturday shift. For such work she receives extra pay, calculated at one-and-a-half times the normal hourly wage. In most instances, she welcomes the chance to earn the extra income.

Maria's working environment consists of a large building containing a variety of working stations, conveyor belts, and other components. During her first few days on the job, she found the area to be noisy and somewhat inhibiting due to all the activity. Before long, however, she adjusted to the situation and now finds it a normal and acceptable part of her routine.

Along with other workers, Maria takes a 15-minute break during the morning and again during the afternoon, along with 45 minutes at lunch. On some days she eats in the company snack bar or a fast food restaurant across the street, and on other days she brings a packed lunch from home.

By the end of a typical day, Maria may be physically tired, but she feels good about her work. It gives her a special feeling of satisfaction to see a finished piece of complex equipment and know that she played an important part in constructing it. When she stops to consider her role as a welder, she feels glad she chose this career.

Welding in Saudi Arabia

For Scott, a job in welding has fulfilled a lifelong desire to see places other than his home state of Alabama. He particularly enjoyed a two-year stint working on a pipeline in Alaska. Scott has worked in California and New Mexico, and now is facing a brand-new adventure: working in Saudi Arabia.

Unlike Maria, Scott spends most of the time working outdoors rather than inside a factory. This has involved a great deal of variety, ranging from frigid wintertime work to the heat of the Saudi Arabian desert. In his current position, he is helping build the towers and other structures needed for a new petrochemical plant.

In addition to the experience of living and working in a foreign country, Scott benefits from the extremely high wages paid to skilled workers in this setting. Along with hourly wages, he earns bonuses, living expenses, and support for travel. A disadvantage is that he is far from friends and family in the United States, but the assignment is temporary, and he plans to return within the next two years.

Typical Tasks

Of course many welders work in jobs far different from those of Maria or Scott, but each position has its own features and responsibilities. Some typical tasks performed by welders holding different kinds of job include:

- Welding joints on the deck of a partially completed ship
- Connecting a steel beam to the main structure of an interstate highway bridge
- Welding components of a cooling system for a new nuclear power plant
- Joining together components of washing machines in an appliance factory
- Helping assemble steel storage buildings in a small firm specializing in constructing storage units and selling them to homeowners
- Operating a welding machine in a truck assembly plant
- Welding pipes in a hospital expansion project
- Repairing broken pipes in an office building
- Assembling components of an airplane

In addition, persons employed as welders may perform other functions as a part of their jobs that do not entail welding itself. Examples on a given day for some welders might include:

- Attending a training session on safety
- Traveling from one work site to another
- Ordering or obtaining welding supplies
- Helping orient a new employee
- Attending a class or seminar on new welding techniques

SAFETY AND WELDING

A major responsibility of welders is maintaining safe work practices. After all, welding is serious business involving potentially dangerous materials and situations. If proper safety procedures are not understood and followed carefully, serious injury and property damage can result.

For example, consider the danger posed by burns. Most welding processes generate intense heat, usually at least several times hotter than the highest temperature reached with a kitchen stove or outdoor grill. If these relatively "cold" temperatures can sizzle a steak, just imagine what a welding torch can do to your hand or arm! And hot metal or other heated material can also cause a nasty burn.

Another possibility is an explosion. If mishandled, flammable gases can cause explosions, endangering not just one individual but nearby workers as well.

Electric shock is another potential danger. An essential ingredient in many welding processes, electricity is commonly utilized by welders. At the same time, its misuse can have devastating results. Failure to use proper safety procedures in dealing with electricity may cause serious accidents.

Welders must also guard against other types of accidents. Eye injuries, inhalation of gases, abrasions, and other problems also constitute possible dangers to anyone working in welding.

This does not mean that people should shy away from welding careers because an accident might happen. After all, most jobs entail at least some possibility of accident. At the same time, paying attention to safety is a major responsibility of every welder. Men and women employed in the field need to learn the safest ways to complete welding tasks and constantly observe appropriate caution in performing their work.

Safety-related responsibilities of welders may include:

- Mastering basic safety techniques within the context of the welding field
- Regularly using equipment designed to enhance safety such as goggles, face plates, and other protective items
- Continually checking equipment to make sure it is in proper and safe working order
- Observing special caution in handling combustible materials and electrical equipment.
- Reading and retaining safety-related information provided by employers or equipment manufacturers
- Participating in seminars or special training programs designed to enhance safety in the workplace

- Keeping work areas free of debris, equipment that is not being used, and other clutter
- Refraining from using drugs or alcohol during working hours or before reporting to work
- Promoting safe working habits with fellow welders
- Keeping safety in mind all the time rather than just giving it occasional attention

QUESTIONS TO ASK YOURSELF

If the life of a welder sounds interesting and you want to pursue this field in further detail, ask yourself some of the following basic questions:

Do I have the right aptitudes? Just as everyone is not cut out to function effectively as a butcher, accountant, fighter pilot, or professional baseball player, every individual does not possess the right traits to work successfully or contentedly as a welder. If you have patience, are attentive to detail, and have good manual skills, a welding career may be a smart idea. If you lack these basic traits, which most welders possess, you might want to consider another area.

Am I dependable? Companies that employ welders need personnel who are dependable. Can you get to work regularly and promptly? Will you work constantly at your daily tasks, placing the importance of the work to be done above coffee breaks, frequent chatting with other employees, and other personal interests? An affirmative answer to questions such as these is necessary for success in virtually any welding job.

Perhaps even more importantly, employees and customers must be able to depend on the quality of your work. It is not enough merely to go through the motions in a job as complex as welding. You must care sufficiently about your work to do a good job, day in and day out. Too much will be riding on the work involved for you to lack dependability.

Do I have the necessary physical traits? People with all kinds of physical characteristics can become effective welders. It is not necessary to be over six feet tall and blessed with bulging muscles, for example, even though physical strength can be an asset in any job involving the movement and positioning of sometimes heavy objects. Individuals who are small in stature or not particularly strong can still function effectively by learning efficient techniques for making the most of whatever strength they do possess.

Some specific physical capabilities are needed, however, and it is wise to ask yourself if they can be found in your own basic profile. Good eyesight, for example, is a must. If poor eyesight is corrected by glasses or contact lenses, of course, it presents no problem. But to perform basic welding work, you must be able to see clearly and be able to distinguish miniscule details in the materials with which you are working.

Physical stamina is also an asset. Welders usually work at least eight hours a day, often standing or crouching. The ability to put in the required hours, which may involve varying degrees of physical exertion, is a routine consideration.

It also helps to possess a good measure of dexterity. This might range from having nimble fingers to being able to climb ladders, squeeze into tight spots, or otherwise move about as the job requires. Depending on the type of job they are doing, welders may find themselves reaching above their heads, lying on their backs, or climbing ladders or scaffolding.

A steady hand is also necessary. Without this attribute, any kind of manual welding will be difficult to perform well.

Am I willing to go to school? To become a welder, you will almost certainly need to undergo some type of training. Although it may be possible to learn the basics of welding under some type of self-teaching situation, it is unlikely. At the very least, most people need some rather detailed training obtained on the job. More frequently, some kind of formal training is needed to land your first job in welding.

Such training can be obtained in a number of ways, including the following:

- High school vocational programs
- Trade and technical schools
- Community and junior colleges
- Technical colleges
- Industry-sponsored training programs
- Government-sponsored training programs
- Apprenticeships
- Military training programs

A description of the various educational options is provided in Chapter 4. Each type of program has its own advantages and disadvantages, but the essential point to establish is your basic willingness to participate in the necessary training. Such a commitment will take up your time and energy, ranging from reading textbooks and manuals or attending lecture sessions to participating in laboratory/shop training where you will obtain your first hands-on welding experience. It may also include a financial commitment on your part, requiring you to pay tuition or other educational costs. If you have not enjoyed going to school in the past, this can represent something of a sacrifice, in that you are once again subjecting yourself to the control of teachers and other elements of an educational organization.

A plus, however, is that welding programs tend to be short and well-defined. Studying welding does not involve going to college for four years and taking a wide variety of courses that may not seem to relate to the "real world." On the contrary, most welding programs can be completed in a few weeks or months, with the longest programs lasting about two years. Because of their occupational emphasis, training programs in welding tend to be as short as reasonably possible and very practical in their approach. This means you will spend less time studying unrelated material, fewer hours listening to lectures, and more time actually practicing welding techniques. As a result, many students, even those who have not previously enjoyed school, find that instructional time passes quickly and that their experiences as welding students are rewarding.

The educational options available to any one person are often a matter of geography. In some areas, several types of welding programs may be offered. In others, a single option may be available. In this case, selection of a training program may mean simply going to one school in your home area that teaches welding. Or it might mean moving temporarily to another city to complete an appropriate program.

Does a long-term career in welding meet my economic and social needs? Any career selection carries with it some implications regarding lifestyles outside the job as well as within the career itself. For example, the salary or wages earned will play a direct role in basic matters such as what kind of housing you can afford or the kind of car you drive. Similarly, job requirements such as shift work, travel, and other factors will influence your daily life in many ways.

Before pursuing a career in welding, make certain that you understand just what type of lifestyle it will support. Be sure to check out income possibilities (covered in more detail in a later chapter), fringe benefits, opportunities for advancement, and job stability. In thinking ahead, it is vital to match your own particular needs and expectations with the realities of employment in welding.

CHAPTER 4

TRAINING FOR WELDERS

In most cases, you will need to complete a special training program to learn the skills required to obtain a job in welding. Although a number of alternative ways to master these skills exist (for example, the special training programs discussed in Chapter 5), the most common path is to enroll in a welding program offered by a school or college. This will involve making educational plans beyond your current situation, choosing a school, and then successfully negotiating the appropriate training process.

PLANNING YOUR EDUCATION

To prepare for a welding career, you will need to plan ahead to obtain the right educational background. In the process, ask yourself questions such as these:

- What schools offer welding programs in my area?
- Am I willing to go away to school, or would I prefer to stay home or close by?

- Am I in a hurry to finish?
- Which is best for me, a trade school or a two-year college?
- How much will it cost?
- How will I pay for it?
- What steps should I take to make certain I succeed?

By carefully considering such questions before you actually enroll in a welding program, you can increase the odds that the program will turn out to be the right experience for you. This kind of advance planning can help you avoid mistakes that can be costly in terms of time, money, and overall career success.

SELECTING A SCHOOL

As a first step, you need to select a school that offers a welding program. This can be an easy decision or a difficult one, depending on the factors taken into consideration.

If the choice is *too* easy, however, it may not be a smart one. Just signing up for the first welding program you hear about or the one closest to your home can be a big mistake. Taking time to select the right school can mean the difference between enrolling in a good program or a mediocre one, or in obtaining a diploma that is widely respected by employers as opposed to one that is viewed with skepticism or disdain. Choosing the right school can also save you a great deal of money.

This is not always easy, but it can be accomplished if you take your time and know what to look for. Unfortunately, almost every school makes claims about itself in an effort to attract students, so you will need to do more than simply read promotional literature or listen to the sales pitch of a recruiter.

Types of Schools

As a basic step in considering any institution, make sure you understand exactly what kind of school it is. Depending on several key characteristics, a school offering welding courses may be operating as a trade school, a technical institute, a technical college, or a junior or community college. Each type offers certain advantages and disadvantages, and you should be aware of them before enrolling in any particular institution.

For instance, a trade school normally offers training programs on a short-term basis in one or more occupational or technical subjects. A typical school of this type offering welding may also teach other subjects such as computer repair, word processing, and diesel mechanics. On the other hand, it probably will not require students to take courses such as foreign languages, advanced math classes, or English courses. When students graduate from such an institution, they do not receive a college degree, instead earning a certificate or diploma.

You can also enroll in welding courses in a two-year college, which might be designated as a junior college, community college, or technical college. In many cases the courses covered will be much the same as in a trade school, with graduates earning a diploma or certificate (usually in a year or less) rather than a degree. In some other cases, though, students complete the equivalent of two years of studies and wind up with an actual college degree, called an associate degree. Students who earn such degrees must take classes in other areas in addition to welding, such as English, history, technical writing, or psychology. Earning any two-year degree will mean completing a few of these courses, which are considered a general education requirement for virtually all college students.

It is also important to realize that many courses offered by two-year colleges can be transferred to four-year colleges and universities. Although this may not seem applicable for welding programs, you never know what changes the future may bring, and you may find yourself wanting to pursue additional college studies later. In that case, you will be a step ahead to have completed at least some courses that are transferrable, such as English and other general studies courses. Courses offered by trade schools, on the other hand, are not generally considered to be college-level, and will not be accepted by four-year institutions.

Of course, if landing a job in welding is your single objective, a trade school may be a reasonable choice. Many two-year colleges offer the same kind of programming as an option to their full-degree programs, allowing you to take welding courses without pursuing an associate degree and the general studies courses it requires. And in most cases, tuition at two-year colleges is much less expensive than that charged by trade schools.

In choosing a school, make sure you understand just what type of school it represents. The name itself may not be an accurate indicator, for some trade schools refer to themselves as colleges although they do not actually offer college-level work. Some others are called institutes; in this case, the school could qualify as a college or might be a trade school, depending on a number of factors.

Getting Accurate Information

Because different kinds of schools offer different features, you will want to know exactly where an institution fits in the overall scheme of things. To get an accurate picture, take a close look at a current catalog for any school that interests you. Look under "degrees offered" or "programs offered," and determine whether graduates earn diplomas, certificates, or associate (two-year) degrees. At the same time, read any descriptions of transfer programs, relationships with other institutions (such as membership in a state community college system), and other basic information about the school as a whole.

Next, look in the catalog's index and find the section on welding. Read the general program description, paying particular attention to such details as what kind of jobs graduates are prepared to fill, level of program offering, length of time expected for completing a program, and similar details.

Take time to read the descriptions of welding courses, which may be found in a different section of the catalog (look under "curriculum" or "course descriptions," usually located toward the back of the catalog). Such details may not be exciting or glamorous, but they will provide a good preliminary idea of the information you really need to make a good choice. Conversely, don't let photos of attractive students or other public relations gimmicks affect your review of this material. Colorful brochures and posters are fine, but their purpose is to make you feel good about the prospect of attending a given school, not to provide the detailed information you can find in catalog program descriptions.

COST FACTORS

In choosing any school that offers a welding program, a major factor to consider is the cost of attending. Tuition, fees, and other costs are rarely consistent from one school to the next. The cost of attending can range from nothing to thousands of dollars. Unless cost is not of importance to you, be sure to find out ahead just what expenses are involved in attending any program.

Schools Run by Public Agencies

Because they are supported by tax dollars, the schools with the lowest costs for tuition and related costs are those run by public agencies, such as a public school system (including both regular and adult education courses), and programs funded by special grants, such as federal job training programs. (described in more detail in Chapter 5). In many cases, programs run by these agencies cost the individual student little or nothing.

Public Two-Year Colleges

Next come public two-year colleges. Such institutions usually operate under an open admissions philosophy and try to keep their costs as low as possible so that virtually anyone can attend, regardless of financial status. Although amounts vary, a typical community, junior, or technical college will charge less than $1500 for a full year of studies. Compared with the high cost of most universities and four-year colleges, this is quite inexpensive. At the same time, even this reasonably low amount can present problems for many students. Fortunately a variety of financial aid programs is available to students who need monetary assistance.

Private Schools

The most expensive option is provided by proprietary schools, privately owned trade schools, and private two-year colleges. These schools tend to cost substantially more because, due to their private status, they do not qualify to receive state or local tax funds. As a result, they must cover operating expenses with higher tuition and fees than those normally assessed by public institutions. At many privately run schools, it may take hundreds or even several thousand dollars to finish a short-term training program in a field such as welding. Unless you have a compelling reason to attend a privately funded school or college, it may be in your best interest to attend an institution that is supported by local or state taxes.

In some instances, of course, the option provided by a private school may still be best. If a public school within commuting distance does not offer a welding program, for example, it may be less costly to attend a nearby trade school than to attend a far-off college or school. Or if a particular trade school has an outstanding track record in training students and placing them in good jobs, it may be worth pursuing training there.

A balancing factor is that students who enroll at more costly schools tend to receive larger amounts of student aid. Since government financial aid programs base awards in part on the average cost of attending each institution, they usually make larger financial aid awards to students attending schools that charge high tuition. It is important to realize, however, that much of your financial aid package may come in the form of student loans, which must be repaid in the years following completion of your studies. So before agreeing to attend a relatively expensive school, make certain you understand the exact extent of financial obligations on your part, both up front and in the future.

REPUTATION AND RESULTS

Cost is only one part of the equation for a successful educational experience. You also want to make certain that you receive high quality instruction. To get an idea of any school's quality, try to find out as much as possible about the school's past record of serving students in fields such as welding. Talk to people who might be in a position to comment on the school's effectiveness and reputation. For example, recent graduates can give you a firsthand assessment of just how well the school served their needs. Teachers, counselors, current students, and employers who hire graduates are also good sources of information about a school or college.

School officials themselves are also a helpful source of information, but keep in mind that it is part of their job to make their institution sound attractive. This does not necessarily mean that officials will be dishonest, but as a potential student, you need to think like a consumer who is about to make an important purchase. In considering any school, look at factors such as these.

Profit-making Intent

Does the school exist to make money? If so, it may operate differently than public institutions. The goal of making a profit may place more emphasis on business considerations than student needs.

Job Placement

Does the school operate a job placement office? Does it work closely with employers? What percentage of welding graduates find jobs in their field? In many cases this figure will be 90 percent or more. In any event, a strong placement service is a must unless you already have employment arranged.

Accreditation

Always check to see if the school is accredited. Holding a license or certificate of approval by the state is not the same as being accredited by a regional or national accrediting body. State licensing often means simply that a school has obtained permission to operate. Instead, see if the school lists accreditation by recognized bodies. For a community or technical college, watch for accreditation by a regional association, such as the Southern Association of Colleges and Schools, the North Central Association of Colleges and Schools, the New England Association, or a similar organization. For a trade school, see if it is accredited by the Career College Association. The latter is not on the same level of comprehensiveness as a regional accrediting agency for a college, but it is one positive indicator.

Ethical Practices

Unfortunately, all schools do not operate in an ethical manner. In looking at any school—particularly privately funded schools that exist to turn a profit—stay alert for efforts to grab students' money. Where there is money to be made, some dishonest people will surface. This happens in education as well as other fields, and every state has some schools that take advantage of unsuspecting students. The most common approach is to "help" the students obtain government grants and loans and then have this money paid to the school even though the students may not receive adequate instruction. In too many instances, schools have closed down, leaving students owing thousands of dollars in government or private loans. Or the schools continue to operate, but students do not receive adequate training and face difficulty in obtaining jobs.

Be alert for such practices. Recruiters for some schools may make everything sound easy and simple, basing their arguments on easy access to financial aid. If you feel doubts about a school, back off before signing anything and check around (with the local chamber of commerce, your school counselor, or the personnel office of a local company that employs welders) to see if the school has earned a reputation for following through on promises.

WEIGHING YOUR EDUCATIONAL OPTIONS

After you have gathered some basic information about one or more schools, take your time in deciding which represents the best choice. A too hasty decision can be a mistake. This is especially likely if a recruiter for a school tries to rush you into signing admission forms or financial aid papers. The smart approach is to refuse to let yourself be hurried or pressured into enrolling.

Obtaining Information

In considering your choice, try to obtain as much information at possible. Read catalogs, brochures, and disclosure statements about financial policies. Take time to talk to friends, educational officials, or others whose advice you trust. Ask yourself, "If I were an employer, would I hire a graduate of this school's welding program?"

Visiting Campuses

It's also important to get a firsthand look at any school before enrolling rather than simply relying on written materials. When you visit the campus, make sure you get a feel for the school as a whole and not just the admissions office. Walk around and look at classrooms, recreational facilities, the library, and the welding lab facilities. Consider whether the school seems to have up-to-date equipment and a pleasant learning environment.

If possible, find out how many students are enrolled in welding courses. That way you can get an idea of the popularity and strength of the program. Bigger is not necessarily better, but a very small enrollment may indicate that the program is floundering and subject to possible termination.

Pay special attention to overall building condition and appearances. Schools of questionable quality often will be located in facilities that are outdated and in many ways inadequate. On the other hand, appearances can be deceiving, so don't base your entire opinion of a school on its facilities. Talk to current students and see how they have fared to date and gather any other information that might be available. You can then make an informed decision rather than simply signing up for the first school you consider.

PAYING FOR EDUCATIONAL COSTS

If you attend a college or trade school, you will need to pay for the experience. Unlike high school, most such instruction will be available only after you have paid tuition and other costs.

The type and amount of costs involved vary not only from one state to the next but from one school to the next. Here are some of the costs that might be charged:

- Tuition—may be charged as a lump sum, per class or per credit hour, or some other way
- Application fees—sometimes required before enrollment
- Fees (general)—sometimes simply called "fees" rather than tuition
- Lab or supply fees—may be assessed to cover the cost of equipment and supplies for welding or other courses

- Student activity fees—often assessed even if you do not plan to take part in optional student activities
- Room and board—for students who do not commute to school, expenses for lodging and food represent a substantial investment
- Health fees—used to support student health services
- Book costs—seldom assessed along with tuition and fees, but you will normally be expected to buy all your own books
- Other fees—separate fees for taking special tests, having transcripts sent to employers or other schools, parking, and other purposes

Of course the greatest cost is basic tuition and fees. The largest portion of your educational dollars will go toward this basic charge.

Financial Aid Available

Although going to school may be expensive, students who need assistance can obtain financial support from a variety of sources. If you need help, you should be able to land a grant, scholarship, loan, or other award to help cover basic educational expenses.

Even though Congress has considered reducing some student aid programs and new restrictions have been imposed in some cases, the U.S. government still supports millions of students through a variety of aid programs. Most states also support their own programs for loans, grants, or other awards. And many private funding sources also provide aid. For students who take the time and trouble to apply for it, a wide range of financial assistance is available.

By supporting grants and loans for college, the federal government tries to ensure that everyone who needs help to pay for college has an opportunity to obtain hundreds or thousands of dollars in student aid. In the process, American students receive more than ten billion dollars in aid from the federal government yearly.

It is true that meeting the qualifications for federal aid can be difficult for families who are not significantly disadvantaged. In other words, the more income and assets your family has, the harder it will be to qualify for student aid. Yet even in situations where financial need is not as great, low interest loans and other forms of aid are frequently available.

Furthermore, individual colleges and universities themselves provide a wide range of financial aid awards including scholarships, loans, and grants. In addition, thousands of private organizations sponsor special aid programs ranging from scholarships to grants.

Plenty of financial aid is available for those students in welding and other fields who are aggressive in pursuing it. If you want to attend a trade school, community college, or other institution, chances are excellent that you will be able to obtain the needed funds.

Qualifying for Federal Financial Aid

To obtain student aid provided or sponsored by the U.S. government, you must first complete a standard application that asks for information about your family's income, assets, debts, and other financial matters. The information is kept confidential, so don't be reluctant to provide such details. They are essential in any decisions that will be made about how much aid you can receive.

This form is known as the Free Application for Federal Student Aid (FAFSA). It is available from school counselors' offices or the financial aid offices of two-year colleges. Or you can write to the following address to obtain a form:

Federal Student Aid Information Center
P.O. Box 84
Washington, DC 20004

You can also apply electronically; check with your school for details.

The application process has been simplified in recent years, but it may still seem imposing. Some families may be reluctant to divulge personal financial information, but the trouble will be more than worth it. After all, just a few hours of effort in filling out forms can bring hundreds or thousands of dollars in grants, loans, work-study positions, or other student aid.

In applying for student aid, be sure to observe application deadlines closely. It is usually best to apply on or about January 1 of the calendar year in which you plan to begin studying in a community college, trade school, or other institution. In some cases, schools may ask you to apply even earlier. As a general rule, the sooner you apply, the better. For some programs, money is available on a first-come, first-served basis. In any event, you can make plans more effectively once you know your financial aid status. The final deadline for most federally supported programs, if you delay applying, is June 30.

Available Federal Aid Programs

Several different aid programs are sponsored by the federal government. Each program has its own advantages and eligibility criteria. When considering them, however, be sure to realize that many students receive awards from more than one program at the same time in a combined package.

Federal Pell Grants

For those who have a genuine financial need, perhaps the most desirable of all the government awards is a Federal Pell Grant. These grants, which were previously called Basic Educational Opportunity Grants, or BEOGs, have helped millions of students pursue a postsecondary education. The great thing about a grant is that is represents a free investment in your future. Unlike loans, grants need not be repaid. You receive the award, use it to pay tuition or other costs, and go on from there without further obligation.

If you qualify for a Pell Grant, you can receive up to $2,340 a year for educational expenses at the school of your choice. This amount will vary with each individual student. Whether you qualify (and if so, how much you will receive) depends not on grades or other factors but on financial considerations, such as the number of children in the family, and parents' income, debts, and assets. Another key factor is the cost of attending a given school, with Pell Grants generally being larger for students who attend more expensive schools.

The main thing to remember about these grants is that if you really need one, you will probably get it. The whole purpose of Pell Grants is to provide student aid to those with the greatest need. So the needier your family is, the better your chance of obtaining a large award.

About four weeks after completing your application for a Pell Grant, you will find out if you are eligible. This will be reported on a Student Aid Report (SAR), a form that you will receive in the mail. This information will also be used by officials at schools where you apply to determine if you receive awards through other government programs.

Supplemental Educational Opportunity Grants

A related program provides Federal Supplemental Educational Opportunity Grants (FSEOGs). Like Pell Grants, these awards do not have to be repaid, but while everyone who qualifies for a Pell Grant receives one, the number of FSEOG awards available at each school is limited. As a result, even if you are eligible, you can miss out on an award under the FSEOG program unless you apply early.

The amount of money available to individual students under this program is even higher than with Pell Grants. It is possible to receive from $100 to $4,000 a year through an FSEOG award.

Loan Programs

If you don't qualify for a grant or need additional funds, another option is provided by various loans either offered by the federal government or made by other lending agencies with government backing.

Perkins Loans

Federal Perkins Loans are available for students who demonstrate exceptional need. Previously called National Direct Student Loans, they provide up to $3,000 for each year of postsecondary study. One advantage of the Perkins Loans is that interest rates are lower than normal bank loans, lessening the overall amount that must be repaid (currently interest is charged at 5 percent). Another plus is that payments may be stretched over a long period of time to make the financial burden less of a problem.

Stafford Loans

Federal Stafford Loans (previously known as Guaranteed Student Loans or GSLs) provide up to $2,625 for first-year students and more for subsequent years. The money is borrowed directly from the government through your school, or from a financial institution such as a savings and loan, bank, or credit union. Because the government backs the loans, the interest rates are lower than with most conventional loans, which makes the loans more affordable. (The current maximum interest rate is 8.25 percent). In addition, one type of Stafford Loan (known as an "unsubsidized loan") is available to anyone, regardless of income level.

Other Loans

Other loan programs are also available. For example, almost anyone with a good credit rating can obtain PLUS loans. These loans are made to parents rather than students. Interest rates do not exceed 9 percent.

Work-Study Program

Many students earn part of their educational costs by participating in the college work-study program. Here, students are placed in part-time jobs, usually at their college and sometimes with community agencies. For example, a work-study assignment might mean serving as a lab assistant, working in the college's library or bookstore, or helping out in an administrative office. Or it might mean participating in a special literacy program in the community as a tutor or clerical assistant.

Students who work in this program earn at least the federal minimum wage. At the same time, they acquire valuable work experience and get to know college administrators and faculty members in a different way than other students. Often, new graduates find their job searches enhanced by positive recommendations obtained from their work-study supervisors.

Contacting the U.S. Department of Education

For more information about federal aid programs for students, contact the U.S. Department of Education.

Federal Student Aid Information Center
P.O. Box 84
Washington, DC 20044-0084

You can also telephone toll-free: 1-800-4-FED-AID (1-800-433-3243)

Internet access at: http://www.gov

Other Sources of Aid

In addition to government aid programs, stay alert for other types of financial aid. These can include:

- Scholarships and grants offered by schools themselves.
- Special scholarships sponsored by organizations to which you or a parent belong (such as churches, civic clubs, lodges).
- Company scholarship programs (for example, the company where your mother works may sponsor scholarships for sons and daughters of employees). Or a local company that employs welders may have established a scholarship fund at your school or college.
- Any other source of aid for which you may be eligible (look through college catalogs, financial aid brochures, and other sources of information to identify them).

APPLYING FOR ADMISSION

Applying for admission to a welding program should not be as complicated as competing for a spot in the freshman class at some prestigious liberal arts college. Nevertheless, certain procedures must be followed even to gain admission at a community college that operates under an open admissions policy.

Make sure you follow these steps when applying for a spot in a welding program:

Apply early. The earlier you apply, the less you have to worry about being turned away because a class has been filled or because some required paperwork is missing.

Provide all requested information. This may include filling out an admissions form, authorizing your high school to send a transcript of your academic record, and similar information.

Get tests out of the way. Many schools, especially colleges, require incoming students to take exams so that they can be properly placed in the right classes. If you are asked to take placement tests or other exams, try to get them out of the way before the school year begins so you won't be held up during the busy period when classes are first starting.

Keep copies of written materials. Once you complete an application or other form, be sure to keep a photocopy. The same goes for test results or other paperwork. That way if anything is misplaced, you won't have to start over.

Be polite. In dealing with admissions officials, always be polite and cooperative. Applicants who are seen as pushy or uncooperative seldom have their applications placed at the top of anyone's list.

Follow up. If you have applied for admission but have not heard anything for several weeks, send a note or letter inquiring about your status. Then when you do receive a response, keep track of anything that is required on your part to follow up on the application.

TYPICAL PROGRAM OF STUDY

When you are considering a school or particular welding course, take a look at the descriptions provided in the school catalog. Or ask for sample course outlines, which are sometimes called syllabi (syllabus in the singular). Course descriptions provide basic information about the material to be covered, including prerequisites—courses and other requirements that must have been completed before enrolling.

Following are some representative course descriptions for welding courses offered by Greenville Technical College in Greenville, South Carolina.

Welding 102—Introduction to Welding. Covers the principles of welding, cutting, and basic procedures for safety in using welding equipment.

Welding 106—Gas & Arc Welding. Covers the basic principles and practices of oxyacetylene welding and cutting and electric arc welding. Emphasis is placed on practice in fundamental position welding and safety procedures.

Welding 145—Field Welding. The study of principles of oxyacetylene and arc welding. Application in the usage of portable welding equipment is also emphasized.

Welding 154—Pipe Fitting & Welding. A basic course in fitting and welding pipe joints, either ferrous or non-ferrous, using standard processes.

Welding 160—Fabrication Welding. Covers the layout and the fabrication procedures as they pertain to sheet metal and structured steel shapes. The course also includes shop safety and hand and power tools.

Welding 170—Qualification Welding. Covers procedures and practices used in taking welder qualification tests.

Welding 204—Metallurgy. Covers the characteristics of ferrous and non-ferrous metals.

Welding 208—Advanced Pipe Welding. Covers study of advanced pipe welding. It also covers the process fit and weld ferrous and non-ferrous materials.

Welding 212—Destructive Testing. Covers the destructive testing methods used in the evaluation of welds.

Welding 222—Advanced Fabrication Welding. Covers the layout, construction, and assembly of metal projects using working and welding equipment.

Most students do not take all these courses, but only those directly related to their program. Some courses are more advanced and cannot be taken until basic courses (the prerequisites) have been completed. But a review of the total listing of welding courses offered by any school can be revealing.

SAMPLE CURRICULUM

Consider the courses that students at Greenville Technical College complete to earn a certificate in welding:

Welding 102	Introduction to Welding
Welding 103	Print Reading I
Welding 104	Gas Welding and Cutting
Welding 105	Print Reading II
Welding 106	Gas and Arc Welding
Welding 108	Gas Metal Arc Welding I

Welding 111	Arc Welding I
Welding 113	Arc Welding II
Welding 115	Arc Welding III
Welding 132	Inert Gas Welding (Ferrous)
Welding 140	Weld Testing
Welding 154	Pipefitting and Welding

Totaling 35 credit hours, this certificate prepares students for a variety of employment opportunities, including jobs in sheet metal fabrication, construction, plant maintenance, underwater welding, auto body welding, and other jobs in the welding industry. As it has a purely occupational emphasis, it does not require students to complete courses outside of the welding program.

For students who wish to earn a full associate (two-year) degree, additional course work is involved. For example, welding students at Northeast State Technical Community College in Blountville, Tennessee, must complete the following courses to earn an associate degree:

Welding 101	Pattern Development I
Welding 106	General Welding
Welding 107	Applied Welding
Welding 113	Fabrication Tools and Processes
Welding 121	Welding Blueprints
Welding 141	Metallurgy and Materials Testing
Welding 201	Pattern Development II
Welding 211	Inert Gas Arc Welding

Welding 212   Pipe Welding
Welding 215   Properties of Special Materials

In addition to these welding courses, Northeast State students must complete the following:

- Concepts of Computers and Applications
- Introduction to Electricity
- Communication Skills for Technicians (or Freshman Composition)
- Humanities elective
- Precision Measurement and Gauging
- Geometric Applications
- Trigonometric Applications
- Introduction to Mechanical Systems
- College and Careers
- Public Speaking
- Social/Behavioral Science Elective

With appropriate training and experience, welders are able to perform the following tasks:

- Read and interpret drawings and blueprints
- Identify and select common metals, filler materials, and gases
- Prepare materials for welding
- Identify, select, and apply common welding processes
- Understand and use both nondestructive and destructive testing and inspection methods

- Weld metals using a variety of positions
- Make measurements and calculations, including strength and loading capabilities of materials

Once you enroll in a welding course, it is best to obtain a course outline or syllabus. Many instructors distribute outlines of this type during the first class meeting. They vary in content and approach, but most syllabi will include objectives of the course, information about requirements such as textbooks or tools, how grades (if any) will be determined, and other important information.

Following is a typical outline for a welding course offered in a community college.

Course number: Welding 110

Course title: Gas and Arc Welding Fundamentals

Lecture hours per week: three
Lab/shop hours per week: nine
Total semester hours credit: six

Course description: This course provides the student with an overview of the basic fundamentals of gas welding (primarily oxyacetylene) and electric arc welding. Both theory and practice will be covered, with emphasis on basic position welding.

Textbook: *Welding Basics,* by M.M. Smith

Required equipment: safety glasses, goggles, striker, pliers, gloves

Learning objectives:

1. To become familiar with basic oxyacetylene welding including flat butt and vertical welding, brazing, and cutting
2. To become familiar with basic arc welding including bead building and flat, vertical, and horizontal fillet welds
3. To master fundamental safety concepts and procedures

Grading scale:

A   90–100
B   80–89
C   70–79
D   60–69
F   below 60

Grades will be based on two exams (40 percent of grade), demonstration of mastery through shop performance (50 percent), and attendance/participation (10 percent).

Topics to be covered weekly:

Week 1: Introduction to course (chapters 1 and 2)

Week 2: Basic safety procedures (chapter 3 plus handout 1)

Week 3: Overview of oxyfuel welding (chapter 4 and 5; handouts 2 and 3)

Weeks 4–5: Oxyfuel applications (chapters 6 and 7)

End of Week 6: Exam

Weeks 7–8: Pipe and plate welding (oxyacetylene)

Week 9: Overview of arc welding

Weeks 10–12: Arc welding applications

Weeks 13–14: Review and practice

Week 15: Final exam

Whenever you enroll in a course, make sure you obtain any outline or syllabus that is available. By consulting it frequently, you can keep the overall goals of the course clearly in mind, as well as keeping close tabs on assignments, deadlines, and other requirements.

CHAPTER 5

SPECIAL TRAINING OPPORTUNITIES

Welding programs offered by schools and colleges are not the only way to obtain training in the field. You can also learn the basics of welding through special programs, such as apprenticeships, government-sponsored training programs, and employee training furnished by companies that employ welders.

APPRENTICESHIPS

A traditional way to master a craft or trade is by serving as an apprentice. As an apprentice, you learn basic techniques by working under the guidance of experienced workers.

Apprenticeships in various crafts have provided career opportunities for centuries. During the Middle Ages, workers who wanted to learn a craft such as carpentry or glass making got their start by becoming apprentices. After serving for a specified number of years and demonstrating competency in the craft area, the apprentice would be admitted as a full-fledged member of a guild or similar organization.

In more recent times, the apprentice system has become less common, but it is still a legitimate training method and continues to be used in many trades. In the case of welding, apprenticeships covering a broad range of metalworking may include the basics of welding. The International Association of Machinists and Aerospace Workers, for example, includes welding as a part of its basic apprenticeship program. The association lists the following responsibilities of apprentices (operating under the jurisdiction of a joint apprenticeship committee composed of members of the union, and the employer) in its *Apprenticeship Training Manual:*

1. To diligently and faithfully perform the work of the trade and to perform such other pertinent duties as may be assigned by the employer's supervisor of apprentices which are related to the apprentice's total training program.
2. To respect the property of the employer and abide by the rules and regulations of the employer, the union, and the committee.
3. To regularly attend and satisfactorily complete the required hours of related instruction as required under this apprenticeship program.
4. To maintain such records of work experience and training received on the job and in related instruction as may be required by the committee.

5. To develop safe working habits and conduct themselves in their work in such a manner as to assure their own safety and that of their fellow workers.

6. To work for the employer to whom indentured by the completion of apprenticeship unless terminated by the committee. Not to seek employment with another employer within the jurisdictional area of this program without prior clearance of the committee, the union, and the employer to whom indentured.

7. To conduct themselves, at all times, in a creditable, ethical, and moral manner, trying to realize that much time, money, and effort will be spent in affording the apprentice an opportunity to become a skilled journeyman.

Working as an apprentice is a time-honored tradition, and for centuries has provided a pathway for newcomers to learn the intricacies of various crafts. It gives you the opportunity to learn skills such as welding under the supervision of persons who have had years of experience in the field.

COMPANY-SPONSORED PROGRAMS

In addition to apprenticeships, which are often run by trade unions, some companies offer their own training programs in welding. They range from formal programs run much like those in schools to informal training situations, where newcomers learn the ropes in a way much like apprenticeships but without strict requirements such as a specific number of hours that must be completed in training.

To find out about company-sponsored programs, check with the personnel office at a company that employs welders and ask if such programs are available. During times when additional welders are needed, newspaper ads may list details about such programs. In many cases, persons who already have experience in welding will be given preference in hiring, but at other times newcomers will be welcomed under the philosophy that the company can train its new workers in exactly the way it prefers, stressing the company's specific production needs.

COMPANY START-UP TRAINING

In several states, special training is made available for new companies or those that have moved to a new location. In some cases, instruction is provided at no charge to the company or the individual worker, thus providing a great opportunity to break into the field.

In South Carolina, for example, the state's 16 technical colleges and the State Board for Comprehensive and Technical Education offer a joint program whereby companies that relocate or begin anew in the state can receive free start-up training for their new employees. The state provides this as an incentive for industry to expand and thus bolster the state's economy; the company benefits by obtaining local workers who are trained promptly and effectively.

For many individuals, such programs furnish a chance to get started and receive training without paying to go to school or waiting months or more to land a good job. Instead, persons who are hired to help start the company usually go through a rapid, intensive training program and begin earning good wages more quickly than through most other avenues.

If a company moved into a new area and needed large numbers of welders, a program such as this could provide training and job opportunities in welding for men and women who had not previously worked in the field. This would be less likely in general welding than in assembly-line work or similar operations, but it does represent an alternative training method in some locales.

MAKING THE MOST OF COMPANY AND APPRENTICESHIP TRAINING

If you find yourself participating in an apprenticeship or company-sponsored training program, try to observe these tips for a successful experience:

Be on time. You can make a bad impression from the very start by ignoring this basic consideration. And chronic problems with lateness can get you into real trouble. The simple solution: always make it a habit to go to work or classes a few minutes early, and you will not need to worry about this problem.

Ask questions. As you begin to learn the basics of welding, make sure to ask questions as they arise. The degree to which you can do this will depend on the personality of senior personnel with whom you work, as some persons enjoy answering loads of questions while others become irritated with too many. You will need to adapt to your own work setting, but, in general, the more questions, the better.

Learn to handle criticism. In a learn-by-doing process, anyone is bound to make plenty of mistakes, especially at first. Don't become upset if your work is criticized—such analysis and comment is exactly what you need. Instead, learn from any criticism that comes your way.

Give it your best. Try hard, and those teaching and working with you will know it. Some people learn faster than others, and if you master things quickly, fine. But if not, keep trying and don't become discouraged. Redo or replace work as often as necessary or put in extra practice mastering specific welding techniques. If you give the learning process your best effort, positive results are much more likely. And the persons evaluating your progress will be more positive about your efforts than would otherwise be the case.

Show respect. In most cases, experienced welders will be older than you. Even if not, their knowledge deserves respect. When you are a student, in a way, everyone else is your boss (or at least is seen as a notch above you). Be sure to realize this and act respectfully in talking and dealing with others. You need not bow down or cater to anyone's inflated sense of self-importance, but try to be uniformly respectful and cooperative with instructors or fellow workers.

Follow the rules. Every corporate training program or apprenticeship has strict rules about what kind of learning opportunities you will receive as well as the limits on work you can perform at each stage of development. Be sure that you know what these rules are and that you follow them closely. Otherwise, you could miss out on key elements of instruction at best, and at worst, find yourself disciplined or even dropped from the program.

Look ahead. If an apprenticeship or training program seems too demanding, just think ahead and picture yourself working as an experienced welder, passing on tips to a newcomer to the field. Remember, any training program will end sooner or later, and the results will be worth all of your efforts.

GOVERNMENT TRAINING PROGRAMS

For several decades, the U.S. government has supported special training programs in welding and other fields that are designed to limit unemployment while simultaneously helping meet the needs of employers for trained workers. Many state and local programs have provided such training through funding from the Manpower Development and Training Act (MDTA) in the 1960s, the Comprehensive Employment and Training Act (CETA) in the 1980s, and the Job Training Partnership Act (JTPA) in the 1980s and 1990s. These and other programs have supported a variety of training approaches, including providing funds for companies or schools to offer special training in fields for which workers are needed.

In recent years, government training programs have emphasized partnerships between employers and educational institutions. This is beneficial to students because emphasis is placed not just on training, but on placing students in jobs after initial training has been completed.

Another plus is that some training programs can be offered by a variety of organizations, not just schools. For example, in many cities, groups such as the Urban League sponsor various types of training. Private companies with a need for more welders can also obtain funds through government channels to hold special, short-term training programs.

Because government programs are designed to make people employable who might not otherwise obtain or hold down good jobs, most have special admissions standards based on income, unemployment, or other factors. To find out more, contact schools or other training providers in your community.

CHAPTER 6

ORGANIZATIONS AND CERTIFICATIONS

Welders seldom work in isolation. Persons employed in the field not only work side by side with other welders, but also participate in organizations related to their professional interests. These groups include labor unions, professional societies, and other organizations.

In addition, welders frequently undergo a certification process designed to assure that their work meets specific standards. Some welders hold several different types of certifications, while others specialize in a single type of welding and thus deal with only one type of certification process.

LABOR UNIONS

Many welders and those in related positions belong to labor unions. Unions, which are organizations in which workers band together to promote the welfare of members of the group in relations with employers, have been an integral part of American business and industry since the 1880s.

Many advancements such as shorter workweeks, higher pay, fringe benefits, and workers' rights have been initiated by labor unions.

Persons employed in welding and related occupations belong to a number of unions, according to the U.S. Department of Labor. These include:

- International Association of Machinists and Aerospace Workers
- International Brotherhood of Boilermakers, Iron Ship Builders, Blacksmiths, Forgers and Helpers
- International Union, United Automobile, Aerospace and Agricultural Implement Workers of America
- United Association of Journeymen and Apprentices of the Plumbing and Pipe Fitting Industry of the United States and Canada
- United Electrical, Radio and Machine Workers of America

As an example of the benefits and responsibilities offered by a labor union, consider the International Association of Machinists and Aerospace Workers (IAM). Workers in this union do not receive separate training as welders if they undergo apprentice training. Instead they cover it along with other content studied during the apprenticeship. At any rate, members benefit from a long-standing, highly successful union track record. Formed over 100 years ago, the union now has chapters in North America, Puerto Rico, and Panama. Its members work in a wide range of industries and hold many different kinds of jobs.

According to the union's publication "Profile of a Trade Union," the IAM guarantees all members the following rights:

- The right to membership in the union regardless of race, sex, or national origin
- The right to attend union meetings (and to speak freely)
- The right to nominate members for offices in the organization
- The right to vote for members for offices in the union, to vote on proposals regarding negotiations with management, and to speak out freely against policies or candidates for union office
- The right to run for union offices
- The right to vote by secret ballot regarding any strike action
- The right to receive strike benefits (after being a member three months)
- The right to receive an accounting of union finances and to be informed on union policy
- The right to propose changes in the union's constitution and to elect local delegates to conventions where votes are taken on such changes

Like other unions, the IAM is financed by dues from members. The minimum amount paid by any member is the equivalent of two hours' wages per month. In return for money paid into the organization, members receive not only the rights listed above, but also benefit from the union's ongoing efforts to attain better wages, working conditions, and employee rights for its members.

For instance, the union might use collective bargaining to seek cost-of-living wage increases, paid sick leave and medical benefits, joint apprenticeship and retraining on the job, pension benefits, safe working conditions, and other benefits and improvements.

The union also works to influence legislation on behalf of its members. It encourages tax reform, enforcement of government safety regulations, and other matters related to the well-being of members of the union.

Unions are stronger and more predominant in some locations than in others. In the industrialized Northeast, for example, labor unions are commonplace. In southern states such as South Carolina, Georgia, and Alabama, on the other hand, unions have never grown to be as strong or as common.

In addition to geographical considerations, union membership may be affected by other factors such as size. Some smaller companies may not be unionized even when large firms in the same area are what is known as union shops. In any event, welders who belong to unions often find the benefits worth far more than the cost of union dues.

WELDING SOCIETIES

Persons interested in welding—whether or not they belong to unions— also may hold membership or otherwise be involved in professional societies designed to advance the welding field. Or they may participate in other related organizations.

The most widely known such organization is the American Welding Society. Headquartered in Miami, Florida, this organization has over 30,000 members. It provides a number of services, including the following:

- Sponsors conferences and seminars about welding
- Supports research in welding-related subjects
- Monitors technical advances and communicates them to members and other interested parties
- Provides information and technical data
- Publishes the highly respected periodical *Welding Journal*
- Publishes *Welding Handbook* and other publications
- Serves as a resource organization about issues and standards related to welding.

For more information about the society or any of its services, write to:

The American Welding Society (AWS)
  P.O. Box 351040
  Miami, FL 33135

Or contact the AWS at its Internet address: http://www. amweld.org

Several other welding organizations, while not as widely based in membership, advance the field through research or provide information of use to persons working in the field. These include:

  The American Welding Institute
  The Edison Welding Institute
  The Welding Research Council

In addition, other organizations prove useful to meeting specific needs. Those who become teachers of welding, for example, may find it beneficial to participate in the American Vocational Association or statewide groups of vocational educators.

CERTIFICATIONS

Even after graduating from an appropriate welding training program, you will need to demonstrate that the work you perform meets certain standards. After all, the quality of work performed by welders is an important factor not only in employer satisfaction but in the safety of property and people. A commercial airliner carrying 200 passengers, a supertanker full of oil, or a 30-story building full of office workers, for example, all operate on the assumption that welders and others who constructed them did a good, solid job in the process.

To help guarantee the safety of these and other structures, government agencies and private employers may require welders to pass examinations to demonstrate competence in the type of welding to be performed. Although the process of taking such an exam may sound imposing at first, it actually is quite helpful to the individual as well as the company or agency conducting the testing. Advantages of the certification process include:

- Safety is assured for all those concerned
- Individual welders learn and improve their capabilities both from preparing for exams and the exam process itself

- Self-confidence is bolstered through successful completion of certification exams

Succeeding on Certification Tests and Other Exams

If you need to take an exam for degree completion, certification, civil service qualifications, or other purposes, be sure to give the process its due while at the same time keeping from becoming unduly nervous about the prospect. After all, welders successfully make it through such experiences all the time.

To do the best possible job, however, you will need to follow measures such as the following:

- If there are written questions, read through all of them very quickly and then go back and start marking answers. That way you have a sense of the overall thrust of the questions. At the same time, your mind can begin attacking more than one question at the same time, at least on a subconscious basis. (Note: certification may rest entirely on an inspection of actual welding work, but written questions may be required in other circumstances).

- If there are time limits, make sure you are aware of them and that you keep track of time. Do not spend too much time on a minor task or section. Also, be sure to bring a watch; a clock may not be available, or it may not be functioning accurately.

- Practice ahead of time. If you will be required to demonstrate certain types of welds and then submit them for inspection, be sure you have spent plenty of time actually performing that type of welding task. The more practice time you spend, the better your work will be. And your level of confidence will be boosted.

- At least several days in advance, talk with a friend, instructor, or co-worker who has recently undergone the same process and obtain his or her insights about the experience. This can be especially helpful for inexperienced welders.
- Don't hesitate to pose questions to the examiner, if that individual is available. This does not mean you should ask them to help you with answers, but you can ask any questions you might have about the exam or certification procedure.
- Don't be nervous. This is easier to say than to do, of course, but try to develop coping strategies. For example, use deep breathing to calm yourself just before the testing experience. Or keep in mind that the future of the civilized world does not depend on your results.
- Learn from mistakes. When you make mistakes, remember that everyone else makes mistakes, too. Instead of becoming discouraged, try to learn from any errors and apply that knowledge to future efforts.

Finally, keep organized records regarding certifications and related matters. In some instances, you may be asked to demonstrate evidence of having successfully passed previous exams.

CHAPTER 7

EARNINGS AND BENEFITS

EARNINGS

Persons employed in welding earn excellent wages and benefits. The American Welding Society (AWS) has studied wages for welding personnel around the country and consequently has made the following estimates:

> For persons trained to perform welding jobs, starting wages across the country range, on the average, from *three to five times* the minimum wage as established by the federal government. The actual amount varies with skill levels, location and other factors.*

Taking AWS estimates and applying them to the current minimum wage ($4.25 per hour), the following wage ranges can be projected.

---

*In some cases, these wages can be as much as *10 times* the minimum wage.

At the lower end of the scale (three times the minimum wage), a welder might earn something like this:

$12.75 per hour
$510 per week (40 hours)
$26,520 per year

At five times the minimum wage, earnings would be as follows:

$21.25 per hour
$850 per week
$44,200 per year

At up to 10 times the minimum wage, the figures are even more impressive. In general, however, wage ranges for welders tend to be more meaningful than average wages, as the figures on which averages are based change frequently and wages can be affected by various factors. Factors that can influence wages include the following:

Location. Workers in urban areas tend to earn more than those in rural areas, for example.

Local cost of living. Wages can be influenced greatly by the local cost of living. In Alaska, for instance, a loaf of bread or a month's rent may cost more than twice the amount for an equivalent item in Mississippi or Iowa. As a result, wages must be higher to compensate for such differences.

National inflation. As inflation occurs at the national level, wages tend to increase—although not uniformly—across the country.

Skill levels. Highly complex welding jobs often pay higher wages than those that require more basic skills. Similarly, individuals who can demonstrate superior skills can sometimes command higher wages than would otherwise be the case.

Local competition. The competition (or lack of it) with other firms employing welders can influence wages. If one company raises its wages, others may be forced to follow suit to avoid losing workers. Conversely, if only one organization has a need for welders, it may be able to offer somewhat lower wages.

Company business conditions. An aerospace company that has just landed a huge government contract may be in a position to offer attractive wages. An airline that has lost millions of dollars may find it necessary to cut wages. The financial health of a company can play a major factor in ability to pay high wages.

Longevity of company. New companies may pay less than more established firms. With less in the way of basic resources than more established companies, they may offer a chance to grow with the organization as partially offsetting lower pay.

FRINGE BENEFITS

In addition to wages, most employers pay a variety of fringe benefits to their employees. These are usually much more extensive for full-time employees than for part-time staff, and benefits vary from one company to another and in union and nonunion environments.

Typical benefits earned by welders include:

- Retirement or pension funds
- Medical insurance
- Paid vacation time
- Paid sick leave
- Workmen's compensation in case of injury
- Social security benefits

In addition, welders in some companies participate in profit-sharing programs, expanded medical coverage such as dental insurance or optical insurance, membership in credit unions, and other benefits. The particulars of any benefit package may vary widely from one employer to the next.

CHAPTER 8

OPPORTUNITY FOR ALL

As with many other technical fields, welding has traditionally been dominated by white males. However, as society and the workplace have changed over the past two or three decades, the diversity of opportunities in this field has expanded significantly. Careers in welding today are open to individuals with a wide variety of backgrounds. Anyone who is interested in pursuing a welding career should be able to follow up on that desire.

WOMEN IN WELDING

Although most welders are still men, increasing numbers of women are entering this field. And their success is opening doors for more women welders in the future.

During World War II, many American factories relied on the work of female welders to take the place of men who were serving in the armed services. Women proved to be excellent workers in welding and other crafts involved in the construction of airplanes, tanks, ships, and other military equipment, along with normal welding functions needed outside the war effort.

Unfortunately, this turned out to be a temporary situation, for when the war ended in 1945, millions of men returned to civilian life and took back most of the jobs in industry. Recent years have seen women developing a new interest in welding careers, however, and more females have enrolled in welding programs and taken jobs in the field.

Some reasons welding can be a smart career choice for women include:

- The pay is more attractive than for many other jobs.
- Many employers will give preference to female job applicants because few have traditionally held welding positions, and companies want to establish better track records in this area.
- Female students can sometimes qualify for special financial aid and support programs, making school or college attendance less expensive or even free. For example, some schools offer programs for single parents and displaced homemakers. These programs can furnish women with counseling services and in some cases pay for tuition, books, supplies, and even transportation and child care.
- Changing attitudes in the workplace and society as a whole have made it less unusual to find women working in technical fields such as welding.

• Women have already proven themselves as highly efficient welders, and any suggestions that men are somehow "better" or ideally suited for welding jobs simply represent outdated thinking.

Of course, as with many technical fields, the majority of workers in welding in the immediate future will probably still be males. But the field is definitely open to women, and more and more female welders can be expected in years ahead.

OPPORTUNITIES FOR PERSONS WITH DISABILITIES

Persons with disabilities may be able to pursue careers in welding or a related area. As with any other technical career, the range of opportunities varies tremendously, depending on the type of disability, the degree to which it is restrictive, and specific job requirements. An individual confined to a wheelchair may not be able to perform some types of welding jobs, for example, but may be well suited for operating a specific type of welding machine. Or a person with a learning disability may be able to overcome barriers to learning and master the use of welding equipment.

Many schools and colleges offer special programs to help handicapped students complete educational requirements and prepare for careers in various areas, including technical fields such as welding. At New River Community College in Dublin, Virginia, special services are provided for students with hearing impairments. This includes interpreting of classroom lectures and other sessions from spoken language into sign language, the assistance of volunteer notetakers who take notes that help hearing-impaired students keep up with the rapid pace of college-level work, and special counseling and support services. A similar program provides extra help for students with learning disabilities. Such services are not available at all schools and colleges, but they are becoming increasingly common. For disabled persons who feel a welding-related career represents a realistic possibility, special programs can make the difference in breaking into the field.

In addition to the special programs offered by some schools, other programs are available to assist disabled persons. For example, vocational rehabilitation centers are located in every state, and they provide a range of educational and placement services. Through these and other avenues, men and women with different disabilities may explore career possibilities and, where appropriate, pursue positions as welders or workers in related areas.

OPPORTUNITIES FOR MINORITIES

Educational and career opportunities for members of minority groups are wide ranging and this is as true for welding as for other areas of American society. Not only do federal laws protect individual rights in vital areas such as education and employment, but many companies make concerted efforts to hire minorities. As employers strive to meet company or government guidelines for affirmative action and equal opportunity, they provide an open door for minority job applicants.

In addition, many scholarships and academic support programs are available to minority students. Almost every school or college has financial aid or support programs that provide students from minority groups with assistance in obtaining the training and credentials needed to qualify for good jobs.

BASIC REQUIREMENTS

Regardless of gender, race, or other considerations, those planning to pursue a career in welding should possess certain traits. The American Welding Society has listed these success factors for a career in welding:

1. Good mechanical ability: Do you understand how and why things work as they do?
2. Logical mind: Do you use common sense?
3. Learning skills: Have you acquired a basic knowledge of applied mathematics, materials, and drafting ... and do you stay up to date?

4. A team player: Do you enjoy working with others? Are you willing to learn from co-workers and able to work under pressure?
5. Imagination: Are you creative and able to visualize a completed project while creating it from a plan?
6. Good physical condition: Have you stayed in good shape? Are you good with your hands, with strong manual coordination and good (correctable) eyesight?
7. Self-discipline and patience: Do you have what it takes to see a job through to completion?
8. A sense of integrity and responsibility: Do you respect the safety and lives of yourself, co-workers, and others? (Welding and joining affect the lives of thousands, perhaps millions, of people).

Certainly some factors may be offset by other considerations (for example, the "good physical condition" mentioned in item 6 would not apply in the same sense to a disabled and a non-disabled person). But anyone seriously considering a career in welding should be able to respond positively to questions such as these.

CHAPTER 9

WHERE TO GO FROM HERE

If after having review the material in this book, a welding career seems challenging, the next step is to chart a path for further development. Such a path will depend on your own particular background as well as your own future goals, but steps in this process might include any or all of the following:

- Checking what kinds of training programs are available to you
- Completing welding studies at the high school level
- Applying for admission to a two-year college or to a trade school
- Applying for financial aid
- Completing a diploma or degree program in welding
- Visiting companies where welders are employed to gain a feel for the work involved
- Completing a company-based training program or one sponsored by the government
- Landing a part-time job as a laborer or helper to gain exposure to welding

- Talking with counselors about prospects for a welding career
- Taking career interest tests or inventories to help establish your interest or potential for this kind of career

FINDING A JOB

Once you finish your education and are ready to work as a welder, you will need to take steps to find employment. Sometimes finding a job is as much a matter of luck and timing as anything else, and in some cases it may require very little effort. In other instances, you may have to work hard just to land that first job. Whatever the case, you will need to know where to locate information about welding positions and how to follow up on that information.

Identifying Job Openings

The classified section of any newspaper continues to be one of the best ways to find out about job openings in welding. Here is a typical newspaper ad for positions in welding that appeared in the Atlanta *Journal and Constitution:*

Welders

Leading manufacturer of railroad freight cars has immediate openings for Production Welders. Applicants should have at least 1 year of experience in MIG welding. Experience in flux core wire helpful.

> Starting pay is $9.50/hour plus a 20 percent incentive bonus. All applicants are required to take a weld test. Position includes a fully company paid benefits program including pension, life insurance, medical and dental.

Ads are also found in magazines related to welding. A single issue of *Welding Journal* listed these openings in its classified section:

- An ad seeking welding instructors placed by a community college (requirements included a bachelor's degree or a two-year degree and progress toward a bachelor's, plus five years of related work experience)
- An ad for a manufacturer's representative, where successful applicants would sell arc and resistance welding machines and systems
- An ad for a service technician to work on machine controls for plasma arc and oxy-fuel cutting machines

Many companies post job announcements on bulletin boards in addition to (or in place of) newspaper advertising. The personnel office will also have such information.

Your local employment service or job service office—provided by state or local government as a free service—also receives listings of job openings.

The placement office of a college or trade school is another place where you can find out about available jobs. Most schools operate such offices with the specific purpose of finding jobs for their students and graduates.

LANDING A JOB

Once you have identified a job opening, you will probably need to fill out a job application. If an application is required, be sure to take your time in filling it out. Answer all questions completely and honestly. Be as neat as possible, and doublecheck spelling and grammar.

A completed application may be followed by a job interview. Whenever you are asked to come for an interview, be sure to take the following steps.

Plan ahead. Before the interview takes place, plan ahead for the experience. Try to anticipate possible questions and practice answering them. Also, try to obtain some basic information about the employer such as number of employees and products manufactured. That way you will be better prepared to ask intelligent questions.

Dress neatly. Even though a welder's position does not require wearing dress clothes, don't make the mistake of showing up for an interview looking sloppy. The old truism about first impressions still has a lot of validity. Make certain you wear clean, neat clothes and are well groomed in terms of hairstyle and overall cleanliness before going on any interview, no matter how informal.

Show up on time. Always be punctual for an interview. Failure to show up on time may make an employer wonder if you will have a problem reporting to work on time.

Stay calm. Although interviews can be imposing, try to stay calm. Remember: even though you may have high hopes about a certain job, it will not be the end of the world if you are not hired. There *will* be other interviews and other jobs. When you realize this, staying calm can be an easier task than might otherwise be the case.

Once you do land that first job, you will be on your way to a career in welding. What's more, you will have joined the ranks of a truly important occupation.

BIBLIOGRAPHY

American Welding Society. *AWS Welding Handbook.* 1991.

———. *Safety in Welding, Cutting and Allied Processes.* 1994.

American Welding Society. *Welding and Cutting Processes.* 1991.

———. "Welding and Joining."

American Welding Society. "Welding: Land of Opportunities." 1993.

Cary, Howard B. *Modern Welding Technology.* Englewood Cliffs, N.J.: Prentice-Hall, 1993.

International Association of Machinists and Aerospace Workers. "Apprenticeship and Policy Manual."

———. "Profile of a Trade Union."

Jeffus, Larry. *Welding: Principles and Applications.* Albany, N.Y. Delmar, 1993.

Rowh, Mark. *Opportunities in Metalworking Careers.* Lincolnwood, Ill.: NTC Publishing Group, 1991.

Occupational Outlook Handbook. Lincolnwood, Ill.: VGM Career Horizons, 1995.

U.S. Department of Labor. *Dictionary of Occupational Titles.* 1991.

"Welders." Moravia, New York: Chronicle Guidance Publications. Occupational Brief No. 27, 1991.

"Welding Engineers." Moravia, New York: Chronicle Guidance Publications. Occupational Brief No. 565, 1993.

COLLEGES OFFERING WELDING PROGRAMS

Many two-year colleges offer welding programs. Over 1300 junior, community, and technical colleges operate in the United States today. Although not all of these institutions do not offer welding programs, many do. To find out if a given two-year college teaches welding, simply consult its catalog or call the admissions office.

Or send a postcard to the central office for two-year colleges in any state in which you are interested and ask for a list of colleges that offer welding programs.

A partial listing of colleges offering welding programs follows. If your local community college is not listed, that does not necessarily mean that it does not offer welding, as this list is not all-inclusive but is offered only as representative information. For any college in which you are interested, contact the admissions office to make sure.

Alabama

George Corley Wallace State Community College
Selma, AL 36702

George Corley Wallace State Community College
Dothan, AL 36303

John C. Calhoun State Community College
    Decatur, AL 35609

Northwest-Shoals Community College
    Phil Campbell Campus
    Phil Campbell, AL 35581

Shelton State Community College
    Tuscaloosa, AL 35405

Alaska

Arctic Sivunmun Ilisagvik College
    Barrow, AK 99723

Arizona

Arizona Western College
    Yuma, AZ 85366

Central Arizona College
    Coolodge, AZ 85228

Cochise College
    Douglas, AZ 85607

Eastern Arizona College
    Thatcher, AZ 85552

Pima Community College
    Tucson, AZ 85709

Yavapai College
    Prescott, AZ 86301

California

American River College
    Sacramento, CA 95841

Bakersfield College
    Bakersfield, CA 93305

Cerritos Community College
  Norwalk, CA 90650

College of the Redwoods
  Eureka, CA 95501

Compton Community College
  Compton, CA 90221

DeAnza College
  Cupertino, CA 95014

Fresno City College
  Fresno, CA 93741

Kings River Community College
  Reedley, CA 93654

Los Angeles Trade and Technical College
  Los Angeles, CA 90015

Orange Coast College
  Costa Mesa, CA 92628

Rio Hondo College
  Whittier, CA 90601

San Diego City College
  San Diego, CA 92101

Yuba College
  Marysville, CA 95901

Colorado

Community College of Denver
  Denver, CO 80217

Front Range Community College
  Westminster, CO 80030

Pikes Peak Community College
  Colorado Springs, CO 80906

Pueblo Community College
   Pueblo, CO 81004

Trinidad State Junior College
   Trinidad, CO 81082

Delaware

Delaware Technical and Community College
   Southern Campus
   Georgetown, DE 19947

Florida

Brevard Community College
   Cocoa, FL 32922

Central Florida Community College
   Ocala, FL 34478

Chipola Junior College
   Marianna, FL 32446

Indian River Community College
   Fort Pierce, FL 34981

Okaloosa-Walton Community College
   Niceville, FL 32578

Santa Fe Community College
   Gainesville, FL 32606

Seminole Community College
   Sanford, FL 32773

South Florida Community College
   Avon Park, FL 33825

Georgia

Bainbridge College
   Bainbridge, GA 31717

Brunswick College
    Brunswick, GA 31520
Dekalb College
    Decatur, GA 30034

Hawaii

University of Hawaii–Kauai Community College
    Lihue, HI 96766
University of Hawaii–Maui Community College
    Kahului, HI 96732

Idaho

College of Southern Idaho
    Twin Falls, ID 83303
North Idaho College
    Coeur D'Alene, ID 83814

Illinois

Belleville Area College
    Belleville, IL 62221
College of DuPage
    Glen Ellyn, IL 60137
Danville Area Community College
    Danville, IL 61832
Elgin Community College
    Elgin, IL 60123
Highland Community College
    Freeport, IL 61032
John A. Logan College
    Carterville, IL 62918

John Wood Community College
   Quincy, IL 62301

Joliet Junior College
   Joliet, IL 60436

Lewis and Clark Community College
   Godfrey, IL 62035

Lincoln Land Community College
   Springfield, IL 62794

Moraine Valley Community College
   Palos Hills, IL 60465

Oakton Community College
   Des Plaines, IL 60016

Rock Valley College
   Rockford, IL 61114

Triton College
   River Grove, IL 60171

Waubonsee Community College
   Sugar Grove, IL 60554

Indiana

Indiana Vocational Technical College–Central Indiana
   Indianapolis, IN 46202

Indiana Vocational Technical College–Kokomo
   Kokomo, IN 46901

Indiana Vocational Technical College–Lafayette
   Lafayette, IN 47905

Indiana Vocational Technical College–Northeast
   Fort Wayne, IN 46805

Indiana Vocational Technical College–Southwest
   Evansville, IN 47710

Indiana Vocational Technical College–Wabash Valley
  Terre Haute, IN 47802

Iowa

Des Moines Area Community College
  Ankeny, IA 50021

Iowa Central Community College
  Fort Dodge, IA 50501

Iowa Western Community College
  Council Bluffs, IA 51503

Kirkwood Community College
  Cedar Rapids, IA 52404

North Iowa Area Community College
  Mason City, IA 50401

Kansas

Barton County Community College
  Great Bend, KS 67530

Butler County Community College
  El Dorado, KS 67042

Coffeyville Community College
  Coffeyville, KS 67337

Colby Community College
  Colby, KS 67701

Cowley County Community College
  Arkansas City, KS 67005

Dodge City Community College
  Dodge City, KS 67801

Fort Scott Community College
  Fort Scott, KS 66701

Garden City Community College
    Garden City, KS 67846

Haskell Indian Junior College
    Lawrence, KS 66046

Hutchinson Community College
    Hutchinson, KS 67501

Independence Community College
    Independence, KS 67301

Johnson County Community College
    Overland Park, KS 66210

Pratt Community College
    Pratt, KS 67124

Louisiana

Bossier Parish Community College
    Bossier City, LA 71111

Delgado Community College
    New Orleans, LA 70119

Maine

Northern Maine Technical College
    Presque Isle, ME 04769

Maryland

Cecil Community College
    North East, MD 21901

Chesapeake College
    Wye Mills, MD 21679

Garrett Community College
    McHenry, MD 21541

Michigan

Alpena Community College
  Alpena, MI 49707

Charles Stewart Mott Community College
  Flint, MI 48503

Delta College
  University Center, MI 48710

Macomb County Community College
  Warren, MI 48093

Mid Michigan Community College
  Harrison, MI 48625

Northwestern Michigan College
  Traverse City, MI 49684

Oakland Community College
  Bloomfield Hills, MI 48304

Schoolcraft College
  Livonia, MI 48152

West Shore Community College
  Scottville, MI 49454

Minnesota

East Grand Forks Technical College
  East Grand Forks, MN 56721

Riverland Technical College
  Austin, MN 55912

Worthington Community College
  Worthington, MN 56187

Mississippi

Coahoama Community College
  Clarksdale, MS 38614

Copiah-Lincoln Community College
  Wesson, MS 39191

East Central Junior College
  Decatur, MS 39327

Holmes Community College
  Goodman, MS 39079

Itawamba Community College
  Fulton, MS 38843

Meridian Community College
  Meridian, MS 39307

Mississippi Delta Community College
  Moorhead, MS 38761

Mississippi Gulf Coast Community College
  Perkinston, MS 39573

Missouri

Crowder College
  Neosho, MO 64850

East Central College
  Union, MO 63084

Moberly Area Community College
  Moberly, MO 65270

State Fair Community College
  Sedalia, MO 65301

Montana

Dawson Community College
  Glendrive, MT 59330

Flathead Valley Community College
  Kalispell, MT 59901

Nebraska

Central Community College, Platte Campus
  Columbus, NE 68601

Mid-Plains Community College
  North Platte, NE 69101

Northeast Community College
  Norfolk, NE 68702

Nevada

Truckee Meadows Community College
  Reno, NV 89512

Western Nevada Community College
  Carson City, NV 89703

New Hampshire

New Hampshire Technical College
  Manchester, NH 03102

New Jersey

Middlesex County College
  Edison, NJ 08837

Passaic County Community College
  Paterson, NJ 07509

New Mexico

Clovis Community College
    Clovis, NM 88101

Eastern New Mexico University–Roswell
    Roswell, NM 88202

New Mexico Junior College
    Hobbs, NM 88240

Northern New Mexico Community College
    El Rito, NM 87530

New York

Dutchess Community College
    Poughkeepsie, NY 12601

Mohawk Valley Community College
    Utica, NY 13501

State University of New York College of Agriculture and
    Technology at Morrisville
    Morrisville, NY 13408

State University of New York College of Technology at
    Delhi
    Delhi, NY 13753

North Carolina

Anson Community College
    Ansonville, NC 28007

Ashville Buncombe Technical Community College
    Ashville, NC 28801

Beaufort County Community College
    Washington, NC 27889

Catawba Valley Community College
    Hickory, NC 28602

Central Piedmont Community College
  Charlotte, NC 28235

Coastal Carolina Community College
  Jacksonville, NC 28540

Forsyth Technical Community College
  Winston-Salem, NC 27103

Isothermal Community College
  Spindale, NC 28160

Mitchell Community College
  Statesville, NC 28677

Rockingham Community College
  Wentworth, NC 27375

Southeastern Community College
  Whiteville, NC 28472

Tri-County Community College
  Murphy, NC 28906

Wilkes Community College
  Wilkesboro, NC 28697

North Dakota

Bismarck State College
  Bismarck, ND 58501

North Dakota State College of Science
  Wahpeton, ND 58076

Turtle Mountain Community College
  Belcourt, ND 58316

University of North Dakota–Williston
  Williston, ND 58802

Ohio

Belmont Technical College
St. Clairsville, OH 43950

Columbus State Community College
Columbus, OH 43215

Terra Technical College
Fremont, OH 43420

Washington State Community College
Marietta, OH 45750

Oklahoma

Eastern Oklahoma State College
Wilburton, OK 74578

Murray State College
Tishomingo, OK 73460

Northeastern Oklahoma Agricultural and Mechanical
College
Miami, OK 74354

Northern Oklahoma College
Tonkawa, OK 74653

Tulsa Junior College
Tulsa, OK 74119

Oregon

Blue Mountain Community College
Pendleton, OR 97801

Central Oregon Community College
Bend, OR 97701

Clatsop Community College
Astoria, OR 97103

Lane Community College
Eugene, OR 97405

Linn-Benton Community College
Albany, OR 97321

Mount Hood Community College
Gresham, OR 97030

Portland Community College
Portland, OR 97219

Rogue Community College
Grants Pass, OR 97527

Treasure Valley Community College
Ontario, OR 97914

Umpqua Community College
Roseburg, OR 97470

Pennsylvania

Community College at Allegheny County–Boyce
Monroeville, PA 15146

Community College of Allegheny County–North
Pittsburgh, PA 15237

Community College of Allegheny County–South
West Mifflin, PA 15122

Community College of Beaver County
Monaca, PA 15061

Westmoreland County Community College
Youngwood, PA 15697

South Carolina

Aiken Technical College
Aiken, SC 29802

Central Carolina Technical College
  Sumter, SC 29150
Chesterfield-Marlboro Technical College
  Cheraw, SC 29520
Denmark Technical College
  Denmark, SC 29042
Florence Darlington Technical College
  Florence, SC 29501
Greenville Technical College
  Greenville, SC 29606
Horry-Georgetown Technical College
  Conway, SC 29526
Orangeburg-Calhoun Technical College
  Orangeburg, SC 29115
Piedmont Technical College
  Greenwood, SC 29648
Spartanburg Technical College
  Spartanburg, SC 29305
Tri-County Technical College
  Pendleton, SC 29670
Trident Technical College
  Charleston, SC 29411
York Technical College
  Rock Hill, SC 29730

Tennessee

Chattanooga State Technical Community College
  Chattanooga, TN 37406
Cleveland State Community College
  Cleveland, TN 37320

State Technical Institute at Memphis
    Memphis, TN 38134
Northeast State Technical Community College
    Blountville, TN 37617

Texas

Austin Community College
    Austin, TX 78752
Bee County College
    Beeville, TX 78102
Central Texas College
    Killeen, TX 76541
Cisco Junior College
    Cisco, TX 76437
El Paso Community College
    El Paso, TX 79998
Laredo Community College
    Laredo, TX 78040
Lee College
    Baytown, TX 77522
Midland College
    Midland, TX 79705
Navarro College
    Corsicana, TX 75110
Odessa College
    Odessa, TX 79764
Paris Junior College
    Paris, TX 75460
Ranger Junior College
    Ranger, TX 76470

South Plains College
  Levelland, TX 79336

Southwest Texas Junior College
  Uvalde, TX 78801

Tarrant County Junior College
  Fort Worth, TX 76179

Texarcana College
  Texarcana, TX 75501

Wharton County Junior College
  Wharton, TX 77488

Utah

College of Eastern Utah
  Price, UT 84501

Dixie College
  Saint George, UT 84770

Salt Lake Community College
  Salt Lake City, UT 84130

Snow College
  Ephraim, UT 84627

Utah Valley State College
  Orem, UT 84058

Virginia

Central Virginia Community College
  Lynchburg, VA 24502

Dabney S. Lancaster Community College
  Clifton Forge, VA 24422

John Tyler Community College
  Chester, VA 23831

Mountain Empire Community College
  Big Stone Gap, VA 24219
New River Community College
  Dublin, VA 24084
Northern Virginia Community College
  Annandale, VA 22003
Patrick Henry Community College
  Martinsville, VA 24112
Southside Virginia Community College
  Alberta, VA 23821
Southwest Virginia Community College
  Richlands, VA 24641
Thomas Nelson Community College
  Hampton, VA 23670
Tidewater Community College
  Portsmouth, VA 23703
Virginia Western Community College
  Roanoke, VA 24015

Washington

Big Bend Community College
  Moses Lake, WA 98837
Centralia College
  Centralia, WA 98531
Clark College
  Vancouver, WA 98663
Columbia Basin College
  Pasco, WA 99301
Green River Community College
  Auburn, WA 98002

Olympic College
    Bremerton, WA 98310

Shoreline Community College
    Seattle, WA 98133

Spokane Community College
    Spokane, WA 99207

Walla Walla Community College
    Walla Walla, WA 99362

West Virginia

West Virginia University at Parkersburg
    Parkersburg, WV 26101

Southern West Virginia Community College
    Logan, WV 25601

Wisconsin

Fox Valley Technical College
    Appleton, WI 54913

Lakeshore Technical College
    Cleveland, WI 53015

Madison Area Technical College
    Madison, WI 53714

Milwaukee Area Technical College
    Milwaukee, WI 53233

Wyoming

Central Wyoming College
    Riverton, WY 82501

Eastern Wyoming College
    Torrington, WY 82240

ADDRESSES OF WELDING ORGANIZATIONS

American Welding Institute
10628 Dutchtown Road
Knoxville, TN 37932

American Welding Society
550 N.W. LeJeune Road
Miami, FL 33126
Internet: http://www.amweld.org

Edison Welding Institute
1100 Kinnear Road
Columbus, OH 43212-1161
Internet: http://www.ewi.org

Welding Research Council, Inc.
United Engineering Center
345 East 47th Street, 14th Floor
New York, NY 10017